W9-BTN-704

Bill -
Stay out of the
way of those trucks!

11/15/00

Praise for
When the Dow Breaks

"Don Cassidy is an analyst of long-standing and of great insight for these heady times. His historical views can save you money—or more importantly help you make it. By reading this book you won't have to personally experience market turmoil to be wiser."

—A. MICHAEL LIPPER
Chairman, Lipper Inc.

"Don Cassidy's latest book is a great addition to his 'eyes wide open' approach to market analysis. He shows how to step back, take a deep breath, and get an unblinking take on the stock market."

—JEFF WALKER
Webmaster
www.lowrisk.com and *www.investormap.com*

"The best investors are the educated investors and Cassidy's *When the Dow Breaks* provides its readers with plenty of historical and technical data to chew on. But more importantly, gives them important insights about when—and why—to sell their securities."

—DIAN VUJOVICH
Author
Straight Talk about Mutual Funds

"Don's central point is well taken: investors *must* understand that markets don't go straight up. So capital preservation is fully as important as capital appreciation, each in its own time."

—JOHN JARES
Portfolio Manager
Berger Balanced Fund

WHEN THE DOW BREAKS

Insights and Strategies for Protecting Your Profits in a Turbulent Market

Donald L. Cassidy

McGraw-Hill

New York   San Francisco   Washington, D.C.   Auckland   Bogotá
Caracas   Lisbon   London   Madrid   Mexico City   Milan
Montreal   New Delhi   San Juan   Singapore
Sydney   Tokyo   Toronto

Library of Congress Cataloging-in-Publication Data

Cassidy, Donald L.
    When the Dow breaks : insights & strategies for protecting your
profits in a turbulent market / by Donald L. Cassidy.
        p.   cm.
    ISBN 0-07-134768-2
        1. Investments—United States Handbooks, manuals, etc.   2. Stocks—
United States Handbooks, manuals, etc.   3. Stock exchanges—United
States Handbooks, manuals, etc.   I. Title.
    HG4921.C355   1999
    332.63'22—dc21   99-28705
                                                                                            CIP

McGraw-Hill

A Division of The **McGraw·Hill** Companies

Copyright © 1999 by The McGraw-Hill Companies, Inc. All rights reserved. Printed
in the United States of America. Except as permitted under the United States
Copyright Act of 1976, no part of this publication may be reproduced or distributed
in any form or by any means, or stored in a database or retrieval system, without the
prior written permission of the publisher.

"The Dow" and "Dow Jones Industrial Average" are service marks of Dow Jones &
Company, Inc.

1 2 3 4 5 6 7 8 9 0   DOC/DOC   9 0 9 8 7 6 5 4 3 2 1 0 9

ISBN 0-07-134768-2

Printed and bound by R. R. Donnelley & Sons Company.

McGraw-Hill books are available at special quantity discounts to use as premiums
and sales promotions, or for use in corporate training programs. For more information, please write to the Director of Special Sales, McGraw-Hill, 11 West 19th
Street, New York, NY 10011. Or contact your local bookstore.

This publication is designed to provide accurate and authoritative information in
regard to the subject matter covered. It is sold with the understanding that neither the
author nor the publisher is engaged in rendering legal, accounting, futures/
securities trading, or other professional service. If legal advice or other expert assistance is required, the services of a competent professional person should be sought.
—*From a Declaration of Principles jointly adopted by a Committee of the American
Bar Association and a Committee of Publishers.*

This book is printed on recycled, acid-free paper containing a minimum
of 50% recycled, de-inked fiber.

To the memory of my late wonderful friend
and Wharton classmate,
Roger A. Powers,
whose humor and incisive thoughts are missed

Contents

Preface

THIS BOOK ISN'T ANOTHER Chicken Little disaster prediction. Your author is not a perennial bear or perpetual doom-and-gloomer.

What, then, is meant by our ominous-sounding title? A recognition of reality! Stocks do not go up forever. They suffer considerable declines all too frequently. This volume will help you prepare for market breaks before they can hurt you badly. Here, we overtly part company with that vast majority of commentators and authors who throw up their hands and intone that all a poor investor can do is vow never to sell and things will work out in the long run.

"Buy and hold," the panacea of money-management firms who hope your assets will remain in their hands, does work. But only passingly and by default. It provides nothing more than a chance for average-at-best results. Unlucky and ill-timed life events, or the very real chance you might panic and abandon your idealistic long-term-holding intentions at exactly the wrong time (right near a market bottom), mean that "buy and hold" can get you only average or less, never better. Are you willing to settle for that?

At some point in your investment career, you'll need to reduce your exposure to stocks' vagaries—in favor of gener-ating higher current income and to lessen the emotional damage stocks' wobbles inflict when you want to feel safe and secure. Even if you hold stocks and equity mutual funds unflinchingly until that transition phase, you will then urgently need to determine how best to perform your partial exit to the sidelines. A total lack of experience in judging market phases and in actually pulling the "sell" trigger will serve you badly unless you get some unbiased help in advance.

You actually *can* beat the market. Doing it is by no means easy. But neither is it impossible, as those random-walk, hold-forever voices would counsel. Advising that you should blindly hold forever, when fierce periodic market storms are known to occur, is like suggesting you wear the same clothing year-round despite known radical changes in temperature and snow depth. Most investors who fail—and certainly all who fail to beat the market fall into this group as well—come up sadly short of potential due to lack of emotional discipline.

Becoming a disciplined investor requires that you learn the history of market patterns (something you'll never get from 12-second newsbites on financial TV) and then also that you study and understand the many psychological forces that drive prices. Stock prices change because traders and investors in large numbers react to news and to the market's own movements—usually irrationally. If you can become an observant and rational participant, you can take huge advantage of the mistakes of the masses. Instead of being a victim and a crowd joiner, you can quietly and self-assuredly stand apart from the madness and profit by your individualist thinking. You can protect capital when the party recurringly becomes too much fun to be safe.

This book recognizes that stock prices always will fluctuate. In fact, you should expect changes in the world economy and in speed of information communication to add to both the speed and frequency of unnerving market volatility. Our thinking will enable you to identify periods when the major averages are dangerously high; that knowledge plus heightened emotional self-awareness will enable you to lighten your exposure. Having less of your money in stocks during repeated and reasonably predictable downturns means you will have more assets preserved for lifelong growth and therefore a more financially comfortable retirement lifestyle. And limiting your exposure to losses will greatly reduce your temptation to panic at bottoms!

The stock market will decline. It produces losses in roughly 3 out of 10 years. Recent highly pleasant (and historically very unusual!) experiences on Wall Street have left all too many investors falsely comfortable about the market's apparent gentleness. You and a million others have learned to "buy the dips." So why not now compound your success potential by also learning to sell the unsustainable rallies? Granted, you have no more chance of selling right at the top than of catching the lowest price when you buy. You cannot be perfect. But does that reality mean you should take a self-designated victim's approach and make no effort to do better than average? How lazy, and how suboptimizing an approach to your investment life! You can achieve excellence and not settle for average. The choice is yours.

This book will show you how to determine when stocks are in dangerously high phases, so you can take action to protect some of your precious capital against approaching storms. It is aimed at those seekers of the superior who are willing to work harder than average to get better-than-average results, rather than merely hope blindly and wait patiently with the masses.

Chapters 1 and 2 lay the factual and important market-historical framework for your new and deeper understanding of stocks' unending movements—cycles that periodically take prices into overvalued and dangerous territory. Chapters 3 and 4, respectively, describe in detail the recurring characteristics of general market tops and then provide a history of actual tops since 1950. Chapter 5 deals with peaks in individual stocks, by discussing both the shapes they take and the events that often cause them. Chapter 6 explains the psychology behind the technical analysis that identifies topping patterns in individual stocks.

Chapter 7 is central: it gives you a psychological understanding of how the market works, of what hang-ups you bring and must overcome, and in particular of the essential virtues of selling. If you cannot sell, you will die with your current portfolio, so all other effort at market excellence is doomed to failure! Chapters 8 and 9 help you to identify and quantify your portfolio imbalances and points of vulnerability and, in response, assemble a right-sized list of stocks and funds for selling. Chapter 10 offers an asset-mix plan for your investment lifetime and then illustrates how to reduce your risk of loss when friendly bull markets have kindly raised your equity wealth above its proper percentage. Chapter 11 makes some off-the-beaten-path observations and suggestions about mutual funds, which have become so many investors' medium of choice. This is particularly important material as more of us become managers of our future retirement nest eggs through 401(k) and similar plans. Chapter 12 deals with that inevitable bugaboo: taxes. If you let them paralyze you, you can stop reading now and retreat to index funds' average returns as a way of life. And you can plan on seeing some great stocks' paper profits melt away as future corporate fortunes decline. There are indeed several clever ways to manage taxes while going about the business of periodically shifting your investments for lower-risk and above-average results.

Enjoy the journey whose road map you now hold in your hands!

Donald Cassidy

1

WHY YOU MUST PREPARE

BRACE YOURSELF: STOCK PRICES don't rise all the time. That may seem a shocking idea to baby boomers and Generation Xers, whose personal experiences and memories of the stock market span no more than the years since 1982. From August 1982 through April 1999, the Standard & Poor's 500 and the Dow Jones Industrial Average each rose 13-fold. More salient in establishing a generation's impressions of how investing works, however, has been the absence of lengthy periods of dreary or frightening price decline. Stocks had risen 55 percent of weeks and 65 percent of months in that wildly rewarding period. Psychologists would call this strong and consistent reinforcement or *conditioning*.

It doesn't always work that way! This book is not one that predicts the end of Western civilization, or calls for a severe bear market and depression, or even one that makes a case that stocks in early 1999 were greatly overvalued. The purpose of this volume is to provide its reader-investors with a balanced perspective on how markets behave over the longer term and, as a natural implication of that knowledge, to offer strategies for dealing with markets that will indeed go down as well as up. The author's hope and intent is that this work will serve as a reference with enduring value rather than being outdated shortly after the century changes.

In the period since 1897, the U.S. stock market has risen 69 times and declined 33 others, if measured in the popular but arbitrary spans of calendar years. That means that in just over 3 of 10 years the market declines. Historical research done by *The Stock Trader's Almanac* indicates that the market rises only slightly more days than it declines: 52.4 percent of trading days result in gains by the major averages. There is in fact an upward bias to stock prices because the underlying economy tends to grow over time. Revenues rise, productivity gradually increases, and even moderate price inflation contributes to rising profits. After-tax profits and dividends are the ultimate reasons that stock prices rise. Undeniably, betting on rising prices *over the long term* is the proper expectation. However, counting on rising prices every week, month, quarter, or year is a mistake. As Table 1-1 indicates, during the period from 1960 to 1999, only one time in five did the stock market rally longer than three months without a month's interruption. Paradoxically, the longer a rally persists, the more likely we are to become sure (incorrectly) that rising prices will continue.

As human beings we are prone to giving overly heavy weight to the most recently received evidence, in what psychologists refer to as *framing*—our (often unconscious) selection of a frame of reference. When prices have been rising, we expect them to continue doing so, in no small part because we can readily cite all the recently obvious reasons that the bull market has been running. Similarly, after a period of considerable decline, we are all very well aware of the adverse factors behind the bear move, and we then tend

TABLE 1-1   Lengths of rallies in months
S&P 500 index, 1960–4/30/99

Number of Consecutive "Up" Months	Number of Runs That Long	Number of Longer Runs	Percent of Runs Longer
1	52	86	62
2	44	42	32
3	15	27	20
4	11	16	13
5	3	13	9
6	4	9	7
7	3	6	4
8	3	3	2
9	1	2	>1
10	0	2	>1
11	1	1	<1
12	0	1	<1
13	0	1	<1
14	0	1	<1
15	1	0	0

Total runs   138

Mean = 2.52 months

Median = 1 < 2 months

to expect continuation or further projection of that recent trend.

This book will offer a sense of balance, reality, and proportion that periodically fades into distant or forgotten memory as long and giddy market rises pleasantly overwhelm our conscious perception. After having read through it, you will have a more balanced sense of the propensity of markets to fall as well as rise, and as a result you will see and be able to implement appropriate strategies and tactics for improving your investment results, and therefore your wealth, at retirement age. Being more in control of your investment destiny rather than feeling like a helpless victim will also make you feel better (which in turn will feed better decision making) along the way.

REASON #1 FOR PREPARING FOR MARKET DECLINES

Insurance companies and their clients deal with two aspects of potential losses: likelihood and economic severity. In other words, what is the chance of being hit by a tornado, and as a separate matter how costly will the damage be if it does happen? As previously indicated, investors' experience since the early 1980s has been inordinately positively skewed. This alone would raise the likelihood that we are underestimating the probability of declining markets, which would be a miscalculation dangerous to our wealth. But a second factor has arisen—one that makes it more crucial to be on guard against declines than in the past. This new wealth-devouring monster is *volatility.* Corrections have become more vicious than in recent prior experience.

As shown in the graph in Figure 1-1, market volatility has been rising since 1992. Not only has actual price variability been rising as measured in percentage terms, but our perception of wild swings has risen: hundred-point-plus days still jar our senses even though they mean considerably less than a decade ago in percentage terms. Volatility may be ideal for successful, nimble traders, but it exacts considerable damage on investors. The more frightening an event, the more likely we are to overreact (selling in panic with nearly everyone else, thus defining a bottom). In addition, volatile markets are likely to turn us off completely and send us to the sidelines, to the apparent but false safety and comfort of CDs and money market accounts. Owning equities, as opposed to long-term or especially short-term interest-bearing assets, is the path to wealth over the long haul, on average. Volatility poses a danger because, at just the wrong times, it drives us out of the stock market. We can either "learn to live with it" or adopt strategies that shield us from its effects. Because our money and our egos are tied up with our investment experiences, learning to ignore market volatility is no more easily accomplished than trying not to flinch upon hearing the screech of a car's brakes behind us.

Why has the market become more volatile, and what are the chances it will revert to its calmer, gentler past personality? Here, the prognosis is not a happy one. Three factors have conspired to make markets more volatile, and these forces seem unlikely to go away. First and foremost, institutions dominate trading. The most commonly cited estimates hold that about 70 to 75 percent of daily trading volume is institutionally generated. As an example, mutual funds had about $5 trillion in assets in 1998, up from $1 trillion in 1990. When a portfolio manager decides to buy or sell a stock, quite often a million or more shares change hands. This huge volume changes prices notably. The trading market for most stocks no longer consists primarily of huge and nearly evenly matched numbers of small investors, each

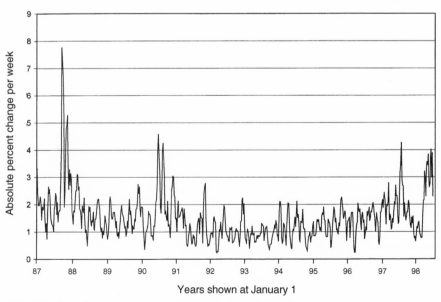

FIGURE 1-1   Four-week smoothed average of weekly percent change in Dow Jones Industrial Average.

seeking to buy or sell a few hundred shares. Ironically, the dominance of institutions (at the time in the form of program trading), cited as one of the contributors to the October 19, 1987, meltdown, generated more rather than less concentration of trading in their hands. Individual investors by the millions threw up their hands and quit trying to manage individual stocks. Instead, they surrendered to the existing environment by joining in as larger buyers of mutual funds. While people have been forced to become their own money managers by the spread of 401(k) and similar plans, that does not mean they feel comfortable with the assignment. So even the individual's need to become adept at personal asset management does not seem likely to turn the clock back on institutional dominance.

Second, and quite sadly, the generally accepted relevant time horizon has shortened considerably. Burgeoning media coverage of mutual funds' every twitch and breath has of course encompassed the reporting of ever shorter performance windows: How did my portfolio manager do for me this week, or yesterday? Ours is an instant-gratification society, and in a period of rising prices we have found short-term performance pleasant to contemplate besides being a natural-feeling thing to expect and demand. The resulting pressure on portfolio managers is predictable: except for the religiously committed buy-and-holders and the true value players, there is no room for patience, no tolerance for under-performers. Out they go! In a dysfunctional cycle of shortening horizons and rising expectations, joining the crowd to dump a stock whose quarterly earnings have "disappointed" the consensus guesstimate by a mere penny per share has become not only fashionable but perceived as necessary. Too many portfolio managers are judged by their relative standings monthly or quarterly, and so they add to the volatility problem by finding it impossible to stick with temporarily injured stocks. Selling begets more selling, and price corrections, once begun, are fierce. You can think of it as the logical and literal opposite of momentum "investing" in that what starts going down is destined to continue doing so. Either everyone wants a stock, or no one wants anything to do with it.

The third factor, which feeds the others, is the arrival of the worldwide age of instantaneous electronic information. Data travels the globe on the backs of electrons. Data hits our computer screens (or, more realistically, some professional's screen first!) and we feel compelled to act in response to its stimulus. The mere knowledge and expectation that millions of other traders and investors are seeing the same new input heightens our perceived need to take action before they do. More information is good, but not in the hands of a crowd of people acting with limited wisdom or perspective.

These factors generating higher volatility seem unlikely to disappear. Therefore it becomes important and even necessary to behave differently now than we did in past decades, when the markets moved at a more leisurely and gentle pace. Individual stocks do literally a year's work (advancing by a percentage equal to their fundamental growth rate) in a matter of a few weeks or months, and sometimes run ahead to outrageously overvalued heights temporarily. One can try to stay calm and remain the intended "long-term investor," unfazed by the wild activity all around, but short of buying an index fund and literally *never* looking at the numbers again, it is impossible to be unmoved. The trouble with volatility is that it is so vivid that it prompts us to do just the wrong thing at just the wrong time, repeatedly. We will succumb to temptation and buy a hot group after it has already doubled or tripled in a few months; we will fall in love despite (or really because of!) its excesses; we will be unable to stand the heat just toward the end of the ensuing price debacle and will sell due to fear generated in great part by the same price volatility operating in reverse.

We must adopt contrarian strategies and disciplines that give us buffers against what the volatile markets would otherwise prompt us to do. We must reduce the negative effects of our frail human tendency to join the crowd. If we all had nerves of steel and could literally and unswervingly hold for the long term, market declines in the interim would not matter. But we are not such superhumans. Therefore we must adopt behaviors that reduce or prevent the injury that we would otherwise allow the market to do to us.

REASON #2 FOR PREPARING FOR MARKET DECLINES

A multimillionaire might choose not to buy auto collision insurance because the value of the loss would be inconsequential in his or her financial picture. Thus, beyond probability and severity of possible loss, we also see the concept of risk relative to the position or needs of the person affected. Not only are the vast majority of individual investors more at risk of actually suffering a reduction of financial comfort than are the superrich, but as you age your sensitivity to declines in the market becomes more serious—in both psychological and financial terms.

In investing, as in sports contests, it's easier to make up for an early mistake than for one in the late stages. The younger an investor is, the more he or she can tolerate the wider variance from "average" that common stock returns provide from year to year. Over the long term, the higher average returns provided by common stocks, plus the fact that stocks tend to rise about 7 years in 10, works in favor of the younger investor even if his or her first year was one of losses. It is that tendency to superior long-term performance *on average, over the long term* that justifies heavier weightings of equities in the early years, as illustrated in Figure 1-2. Here, the so-called Rule of 110 is displayed: an investor should maintain a percentage equities representation of at least the difference between 110 and his or her current age. One might think of this lifelong formula for asset allocation as a glide path toward a reasonably smooth landing. Using the rule's guidance, at age 65 a person reaching or contemplating retirement would have only 45 percent of capital exposed to the potentially violent moves that stocks make. If, at that time, stocks were to suffer a sudden 25 percent decline, only 10.2 percent of total capital (11.25 out of 110) would be lost, and that only on paper. If income from the whole remaining principal were insufficient for living expenses, our hypothetical investor could dip slightly into capital; based on history it would be likely that the market's decline would be recovered in a few years.

A much deeper reduction of overall capital would have occurred if the nearly retired investor had remained entirely or heavily positioned in stocks. One should invest mainly for growth early, and mainly for income later, with a gradual feathering of the engines along the way—rather than making a sudden, radical shift at some arbitrary age milestone. What if you had planned a sharp reduction in your stocks position at age 64, only to have a major market decline hit six months before that? Would you have the courage to keep your stocks for recovery, and the energy and will to perhaps delay actually retiring until the market had rebuilt the capital from which you'd planned to draw a retirement income? Most of us would say "better safe than sorry," and opt for reducing our chances to get rich rapidly after about age 60 in favor of

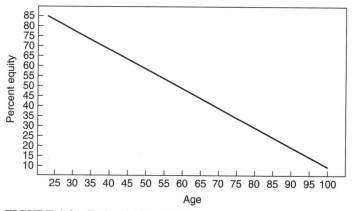

FIGURE 1-2   Rule of 110 graph.

virtually eliminating our risks of becoming suddenly poor at that time.

Although it may sound simplistic, the best way to avoid losing money to a decline in stocks is to sell stocks while they are still up. No, you will definitely not sell out at the top, and no, it would not be a great idea to sell all your stocks at once. In the same way that dollar cost averaging reduces your average purchase price, value averaging increases your average selling price. The practice of taking some money off the table just when it seems most fun to remain in the game at full tilt is one that serves well throughout life. But in the later glide-path stages, especially with a volatile stock market as the likely scenario, preparing for a declining market before one has actually begun is even more important. A side benefit is that you will sleep more soundly by knowing that even in a historically unlikely severe stock market dive only a small portion of your total assets could be washed away on paper.

REASON #3 FOR PREPARING FOR MARKET DECLINES
It is a general principle in life that acting according to a plan, thought out in advance, works better than reacting to events as if they could never have been predicted. Stocks decline as well as advance, and their declines tend to be more rapid in point or percentage terms than their rises. Fear is simply a stronger emotion than greed, and it more often drives us to literally irrational behavior. This is another reason it is better to sell some stocks on the way up—yes, before the market tops out—than to try to sell on the way down. Aside from the potential for an overcommitted investor to panic and sell just as an emotional bottom is forming, there is also the framing issue again.

Suppose you had bought a stock at 10 and it has risen to 50. You now see trouble ahead for the company, its industry, or the economy—or maybe just sense a general correction in stocks is about due. If you have taken care of the hang-ups about taxes that will be covered in Chapter 12, you will be reasonably well able to sell your stock at 50. But suppose instead that you bought the stock at 10 and saw it rise all the way to 100, only to then hold on as a sickening decline back to 50 took place. In this situation, your view of the stock is framed much differently: you see not the gain from 10 to 50, but the loss from 100 to 50 most sharply. Because the stock once (and perhaps not too long ago!) traded at 100, you see it as "worth" that price and yourself as deserving of having that former lofty status restored. It is much more difficult to sell now at that same price of 50 than it would have been on the way up. The principle applies just as validly at a price of 90 or 80 as at 50. Psychologically, we strongly prefer not to lose. We "value" a loss of a given amount about twice as highly as a gain of the same amount. It is more difficult or painful to give up the 10 points from 100 down to 90 than to give up the *chance* of another 10 points never yet experienced by selling at 90 on the way to 100.

It is simply better to sell (and buy) early rather than late. The reason lies in our behavior after having realized the mistake of overstaying. At first, as prices decline, we will believe the price drop to be only another periodic correction in a bull market not yet completed. At some point, however, and this may not occur until a loss in the 25+ percent range has already taken place, we will realize a bear market is in process. Starting *then,* we must work on overcoming the framing problem to sell our stock for much less than we earlier "could have, should have." It is very likely that this process of admitting our imperfection will extend into the last phases of the market's decline. At some point, we might dig in our heels and refuse to sell at such ridiculous new bargain levels. Would that our resolve would hold! All too likely, we will eventually succumb to panic near or right at the bottom, selling much too late instead of slightly late and slightly below the highs.

Selling too late just sets up the next mental trap for us. We have just suffered painful injury, both to our finances and to our fragile egos. Stocks are now a scary thing for us, and we need to have some time and space to heal our wounds. So we stash the dollars we salvaged in a CD or a money market fund while stocks battle to form a bottom. Each decline reinforces our comfort at no longer being exposed to stocks' risk. We imagine each rally as only a false move bound to become a trap before a renewed, even more savage, decline. It will take us some time to rebuild a comfort zone about being invested in stocks. Meanwhile, because stocks rise about 70 percent of years, the odds favor the market's rebounding while we remain on the sidelines seeking emotional safety and rebuilding our courage.

Thus, the original error of not selling somewhat early leads first to selling much too late (and considerably lower), and that horrifying experience leads to our buying late and missing out on a serious part of the ensuing rebound and bull market. It can get even worse: having entered the upswing late, we will perceive the bull market as being shorter than it actually is, and therefore will be unlikely to sell out soon in the belief that "this up market has been too short to end yet." All of this because we made the error of overstaying a market top that may now be three to five years in the past. We have thrown ourselves seriously out of sync, or off cycle, with the market and have lost several years' time in building capital as a result.

As we journey deeper into our investing careers and have fewer years to repair mistakes, and *because* markets are more volatile and therefore more dangerous than they used to be, it is more crucial than ever to anticipate market downturns and judiciously take some chips off the table before a losing streak sets in.

FROM THE THEORETICAL TO THE PRACTICAL

This chapter has dealt with the broad theory behind fluctuating markets and cyclical behavior as a reason for becoming a proactive investor who learns to sell the rallies as well as buy the dips.

Chapter 2 will take you on a quick replay of history. There, you will see the actual declines of the past—their depth and frequency—and will appreciate more clearly how often stock market downturns occur and how serious their losses typically become. The period from 1982 to the time this was written was truly an extraordinary time, and one that really should not be taken as the norm. Stocks do indeed rise most of the time, but not all of the time. As you descend further along your personal glide path, can you afford to make the wrong assumption and overstay a bull market? Only if you are literally so wealthy that you needn't worry about it can you take the chance of being wrong and *not* preparing for the market's recurring declines.

So, let us review history, lest we be doomed to blindly repeating it.

2

A HISTORY
OF MARKET BREAKS

MARKETS **DO** **NOT** **MOVE** in the same direction forever. Please reread that! Emotions carry prices periodically above, and then below, levels justified by fundamentals. True, in the long run, fundamentals such as supply and demand determine prices of commodities and money: earnings and dividends and cash flows determine the values of stocks. But in the interim (before we ever arrive at that always-elusive long-term point), emotions drive prices.

It will always serve you well to think carefully about the difference between the words *value* and *price*. The former refers to intrinsic qualities and quantities, while the latter is merely the momentary level at which buyers and sellers are doing business. The final third of the twentieth century saw booms and busts in silver and gold, in oil and other energy prices, in real estate, and in both bonds and stocks. Prices moved a great deal in relatively short periods of just a few

years. Underlying values, when one looks back in the cool-
ness of 20/20 hindsight, did not change nearly as much as the
transaction prices did. Prices overshot, alternately, on the
high and then on the low side. It happens over and over again
in any free or primarily free market. It will continue that way
until human nature changes.

This book is about being more successful than average in
your investment life. It is about being different, about stand-
ing back and watching the crowd and being careful not to
join it in the latter stages of its predictable and repeated
manias and panics. Our thesis is that one can indeed do better than average. This runs 180° into the face of all the popular press articles that recite the gospel of passive, "forever"
investing. In order to do better than average in equities
(which is about 11 percent a year but hardly ever very close
to 11 percent in any single year), you must be something
other than a passive participant in the markets.

Long-term buying and holding can work, but only if you
never have a personal need such as education expenses,
unemployment periods, or uninsured medical setbacks—and
only if you never let your emotions drag you out of the market after a painful decline or entice you into the market up to
your eyeballs when it has already become frothy and fun. So,
if you are lucky enough never to face those financial crises
and absolutely disciplined enough always to avoid following
the crowd, and if you are satisfied with getting merely average results for your efforts over the long term—then go
ahead and be passive. And save yourself any further expense
or effort related to getting a financial education: buy a major
index fund and absolutely never, never do anything but hold
it until you die or retire, whichever comes first.

For the rest of us, there is a world of opportunity and risk
out there to be dealt with. A world in which markets move to
silly heights every few years, and then just as predictably
will fall off to panicky lows, only to recover again. For us,
the markets represent the challenge and opportunity of not

settling for "just average." Outperforming the long-term average returns of the stock market requires four essential elements:

1. A knowledge of market history that provides perspective on the present

2. A disciplined emotional framework that keeps us from falling into the traps of current fads (positive or negative)

3. Decisiveness, allowing us to act (selling as well as buying) when we see the signs we expected and awaited

4. An acceptance of our own fallibility, which allows us to reject the paralyzing effects of perfectionist behaviors

This chapter will give you historical information on the U.S. stock market. It is absolutely true that history does not repeat itself exactly. But as one veteran market colleague said, it does tend to rhyme. While successive patterns and cycles do not display exactly the same amplitude or time dimensions, I can assure you from a lifetime of experience that it is better to know a lot about history than to be ignorant of it. Fairly good, albeit imprecise, guides that have a history of working more times than not are very valuable. Flying blind is just too risky.

Critics, you may observe, say that anything other than buying and holding passively forever is "market timing," and they say that this cannot be done successfully. (Many academics start with the assumption that markets move randomly, crunch reams of data in which they do not perceive patterns, and pronounce the markets random and therefore unbeatable. Most such researchers, if indeed they venture out of the confines of the ivory tower, are timid and passive investors rather than proactive competitors in the marketplace. Their own mediocre results are all the proof they need—or want!—that no one could do any better than they have.) This author fully agrees that market timing, in the sense of predicting future moves, is difficult. Difficult yes, but not impossible. Some degree of success beyond just average is a realistic goal if one is armed with the lessons of market history!

My approach is to observe what the market has done already, to assume that trends will again become overdone as they have in the past, and to take counterbalancing action *after* price moves have already been either lengthy in time or extreme in extent. Rather than trying to pick exact tops or bottoms, my approach—which underlies the suggested wealth-building and -retention actions in this book—is to look through the past as a lens into the present and run the other way when classic signs of extremes are visible.

Markets do not move in one direction forever. Nor do they move only slightly, in exact parallels with moderate changes in gross domestic product (GDP) or earnings per share (EPS). Rather, markets move between extremes of over- and undervaluation. It is not easy to predict the future in a vacuum, but it is not at all impossible to observe the recent past and thereby discern when change rather than continuation of its trends is probable. I operate on the basis of probability-supported, reasonable (which means contrarian) responses to observed past phenomena, rather than courageously but blindly trying to predict the future devoid of any context.

WHAT DO WE KNOW FROM HISTORY?

First, we know from even a casual glance at any long-term historical chart that stock prices do not move up in an uninterrupted straight line. In the twentieth century, stocks rose in about 7 out of 10 years—unfortunately, not exactly in 7 out of each 10 years. Would that the investing world were that simple! Stock prices have declined by 10 percent or more, using the major averages as a measure, some 53 times, or on average one time per two years—but again, not exactly once in *each* two years. The decline from July to October 1998 once again brought out an amusing but totally useless semantic exercise, in which participants debated what percentage of decline constitutes a "correction" and what extent qualifies as an official "bear market." What difference does a label make? I would hope that if the debate were ever definitively resolved, meaning that a bear market "officially" became a decline of more than exactly X percent, people would have the good sense to ignore the tolling of the official village bell. Once the decline has become large enough to become an official bear, what should you do? Certainly it is already too late to sell! What, then, is the use of these labels other than as media dramatics?

Setbacks of 10 percent or more in the popular averages, coming a little more than once per two years, are only part of the story of market declines. Indeed, in the twentieth century there were 15 drops of 25 percent or more—on average, but not with perfect rhythm, one per six to seven years. It has long been observed that U.S. stocks seem to display a cycle length of approximately four years (although not precisely 48 months!), just about equal to the presidential election term. (See Table 2-1.) Whether there is a cause-effect relationship is debatable, but the fairly regular appearance of market bottoms roughly four years apart is indisputable. If there are bottoms that often, and if there were 53 declines of 10 percent or more (including the 15 of over 25 percent!), then there have also been at least one and probably two toppy periods in the market per four years . . . times when it will have proved to be very worthwhile to lighten up on stocks and thereby preserve assets. Another way of visualizing the data is to think in 12-year time windows: on average, such a span of years will contain four declines of 10 percent or more and another two of 25 percent or more. Now how warm and cozy do you feel about those passive, hold-forever strategies that are so widely touted?

TABLE 2-1   A half century of bottoms about every four years

Date of Low	Years Apart	DJIA at Bottom
June 1949	—	161
Sept. 1953	4	254
Oct. 1957	4	413
June 1962	5	525
Oct. 1966	4	736
May 1970	4	627
Dec. 1974	4	571
Mar. 1978	4	737
Aug. 1982	4	770
Oct. 1987	5	1739
Oct. 1990	3	2635
Nov. 1994	4	3739
Aug. 1998	4	7400

WHAT CAUSES STOCK MARKET DECLINES?

Declining corporate profits, strongly rising inflation rates, and significant external factors such as wars and cataclysmic natural events (earthquakes, famines, devastating storms, and the like) are fundamental drivers that cause stock prices to decline. If you have any doubt that corporate earnings drive value over the long term, consider this: in the twentieth century, corporate profits grew very irregularly but at a net average annual rate of 9 percent. Add a couple of percent for dividends paid out, and you arrive at the widely quoted 11 percent total return for stocks documented by Ibbotson Associates.

But back to declines and their triggers: sometimes stocks decline without any major trigger. Sometimes just the fact that they have advanced for a long time and by a large percentage means that their prices have run far ahead of value and therefore a retrenchment is required. (Hesitant, value-conscious buyers must be tempted by lowered prices.) Too much partying creates a hangover and a painful headache. Like an incurable party animal, the stock market never quite seems to overcome its tendency to binge and then pay the price; it cannot seem to live on a narrow course or an even keel.

In that fact of investment life lie both challenge and opportunity. In business it is widely agreed that keeping an old customer is easier and less costly than winning a new one. Likewise with investing in stocks, it is very important to preserve capital after gains have accrued. Lost money, whether it be 10 percent, 25 percent, or more, is lost time. And time is all an investor has. As you approach the glide-path phase of life, capital preservation becomes more critical with each year and each price cycle. But, also of major importance, early-life success in avoiding the passive investor's full cycle of gain and loss and recovery will create an immensely larger asset pool to work with later on.

When stocks have risen too far too fast to be able to sustain their new lofty heights, one or two things have repeatedly happened. Fundamentally, prices have risen much more than corporate earnings, meaning that price-to-earnings (P/E) ratios have expanded—probably into the range that characterized prior toppy periods in market history. Or, psychologically, a lengthy and large rise in prices invites speculation, decreases inhibition about risk, and also draws in the previous sideline dwellers. When comfort pervades and then excitement rises to a fever pitch, literally everyone who will become willing to play the game finally has already joined the fun. There is no new money left to drive prices higher. There might be a frightening news development, or perhaps buyers will simply run out of gas. The first sharp correction begins a process of breaking the speculative fever. The continuing decline snuffs out enthusiasm and optimism, and in the end all remaining confidence will be dashed in a panicky selling climax. (Thus the sage advice of Ralph Acampora: if you're going to panic, do it early!)

Tops can and often do occur without good economic reason. Markets are said to forecast the economy's future. But the frequency of significant price declines has spawned an old investment cliché that the stock market has forecast 12 of the past 5 recessions. Market tops, coming frequently, are a fact of life. You can choose to suffer repeatedly from their aftereffects, or you can learn to anticipate them and take protective action.

As noted previously, while tops occur frequently, they do not come with total regularity. But their frequency raises the idea that a lengthy rise can be said to be "living on borrowed time." Here we think in terms of runs of consecutive rises and falls, whether they be counted in terms of days, weeks, months, quarters, or years. Table 2-2 traces consecutive annual rises, indicating how unusual uncorrected-gain streaks become in relatively short order. For example, slightly under half the upward runs extended beyond two calendar years, and only 6 in 25 ran longer than three years. The good news is that the vast majority of declining streaks fail to extend for as long as two years. The two longest decline streaks occurred during the Great Depression (four years) and in World War II (three years).

History is of mere academic amusement unless its lessons are applied. Knowing, from the material just presented, that an advance of more than so many consecutive months, quarters, or years is among the longest ever seen tells you when holding stocks is putting your wealth on "borrowed time." The next month or quarter might provide further gains, but the odds begin to favor a correction once the advance has persisted longer than average. Remember this, too: good news will abound after a long rise. Everyone will know all the reasons that have supported the heroic climb. You must ignore the celebration over fundamentals and focus on the psychological factors, which will show classic toppy signs.

TABLE 2-2   Annual runs, twentieth century

Length in Calendar Years	Up Markets		Down Markets	
	Number of Runs	Percent of Runs Longer	Number of Runs	Percent of Runs Longer
1 year	2	92	18	25
2	12	44	4	8
3	5	24	1	4
4	3*	12	1	0
5	2	4	0	0
6	1†	0	0	0
Total	25		24	
Years up/down: 69/33 in 102				

*Includes 1995–1998 run which might extend.
†Includes six-year run of 1897–1902.

SEEKING A ZONE OF DISCOMFORT IS REQUIRED

One psychological or behavioral observation in relation to the lessons of history is central: successful investing requires doing what is uncomfortable, not what has already become "obvious" and easy. In the late stages of a market advance, you will be highly aware of all the good news and will be enamored of your portfolio holdings. Everyone will be having fun on Wall Street and Main Street. In such an atmosphere, it will feel strange and lonely to not continue in the game. You will feel strongly tempted to continue participating for just a little more upside, because winning will seem so easy and continuing to play will appear the obvious best bet. But try very hard to be objective and rational: your job is to reduce risk and protect assets for a secure retirement.

You should not expect to get rich rapidly or consistently; you should expect significant market declines to occur—and not infrequently. You should expect to feel uncomfortable in selling early, when everyone around you is still buying and trading and celebrating. If instead you wait until it is obvious that something has gone wrong and a major decline is already in process, you will have made a mistake and more than likely will sell near the next bottom rather than only slightly after the last top. Selling in panic is a means of seeking comfort, and so is holding in a heady, giddy, toppy market climate. You must cultivate an ability to do what is lonely and uncomfortable in the market. History will be on your side, but at the time you take action it will not be quite obvious just yet. Expect to feel uncomfortable.

SUMMARY

This chapter has provided a primarily quantitative historical perspective on the stock market's tendency to advance and then decline in frequent but not precisely rhythmic cycles. We've also alluded to some of the most commonly cited causes of market declines, while still noting that not every decline necessarily has any logical cause. We've concluded with some advice about emotional control that must be adopted if investors are to avoid the trap of holding forever and thereby giving back large parts of the gains garnered from each bull market.

Some declines mysteriously begin when least expected. In Chapter 3 we will focus on some measures that often precede and signal tops. Perhaps more important, however (because investing is an art rather than a science and because emotions and psychology hold sway in the medium term), the following pages will offer a catalog of softer things: moods, attitudes, conditions, and observations you can note as a market rises. No one of them alone is a final signal of a top, but a large accumulation of these is usually a strong signal of trouble not far ahead! So, onward from history to observing the present with perception.

3

IDENTIFYING GENERAL MARKET TOPS

N**O TWO MARKET CYCLES** are the same. That's true in terms of time, amplitude, and character. No two market highs are exactly the same: P/E ratios and average yields do not hit exactly the same levels and then turn around. Look for readings in the historically known higher *range* rather than focusing rigidly on some precise number. Leading individual stocks, likewise, never can be expected to top out at exactly the same valuation levels as in the past. Signs of a dangerously high stock market are seldom novel, because both fundamental and psychological patterns repeat! In this chapter we will provide some actual data on past cyclical tops, but we will concentrate on typical *patterns* you should expect to observe—and these are more general and behavioral than precisely mathematical in nature. Sorry, you would-be market scientists: it just does not work the exact same way time and again! The broad outlines repeat, but the details never do.

HIGH P/E RATIOS AND LOW YIELDS

Let us begin by looking at the valuation history of bull-market highs during the past half century or so. Table 3-1 indicates that markets have topped out when price/earnings ratios were at a wide range of levels—from as low as 9× in 1981 to above 20× on several occasions. So P/Es alone seem to provide little of the desired but elusive precise guidance in determining "how high is high." Another well-worn rubric is to beware of average dividend yields that fall below 3 percent. But as the data indicate, nearly half the high-market years provided yields of 3.1 percent or higher, while recent years have seen bull markets run considerably further than the 3 percent level. Again, not much help.

What does seem interesting—and is logically relevant— is the relationship of both P/E ratios and dividend yields to

TABLE 3-1   Valuation measures at past major market highs

High Year	S&P 500 High P/E	S&P 500 Low-Dividend Yield	Long-term U.S. Treasury Bond Average Yield	Ratio: Dividend-to-Bond Yield
1947	22×	4.8%	2.24%	2.14×
1956/7	14	3.6	3.26	1.10
1959	18	3.1	4.10	0.76
1962	22	2.9	3.95	0.73
1965	17	3.1	4.68	0.66
1969	17	3.1	6.22	0.50
1972	18	2.7	5.67	0.48
1976	12	3.6	7.87	0.46
1981	9	4.6	13.20	0.35
1987	21	2.7	8.76	0.30
1990	16.8	3.26	8.81	0.37
1993	21.3	2.70	6.46	0.42
1997Q4	24.2	1.60	6.27	0.26
1998Q3	29.7	1.38	5.81	0.24

the level of yields on long-term government bonds. Here, we make two observations. First, P/Es and government bond yields cannot both be high. High yields on bonds represent tough competition for stocks. The year 1981 was a classic example; stocks were too high even at single-digit P/Es, when you could nail down 13+ percent yields and a chance for capital recovery in bond prices. By contrast, 1947 saw bond yields of well under 3 percent, so P/Es were able to soar. The second observation is the changing relationship between dividend and bond yields: stocks have been yielding ever less relative to bonds over time. The period before 1960 was one in which, amazing at it now seems, investors demanded higher yields from stocks than from bonds. Why? Probably because of recent memories of vicious stock price declines and dividend cuts/omissions during the 1930s. Thus, stocks were viewed as relatively risky until about 1957 and have been seen as increasingly desirable since then.

The late 1990s brought frequent assertions that "it's different this time," because companies are buying back stock rather than paying out as high a percentage of earnings as previously. That observation is supposed to make minuscule dividend yields acceptable—and after all, high dividends are tax-inefficient. If one grants that perhaps this thinking is valid because the rise in P/E ratios is nowhere near as severe as the drop in dividend yields, two key factors arise. That is, the 1998-type level of valuation (very low yields and historically high P/E ratios) depends on continuance of two critical ingredients: earnings must not decline, and perhaps even more critically, inflation (driving yields) must not increase.

To remain comfortable with late-1990s levels of general market valuation, you are by implication *assuming* that interest rates will not rise from current levels. While economic prospects as we go to press seem to support that outlook, low rates' continuance is absolutely critical to averting a serious

decline in stock prices. Absent a dramatic decline in corporate tax rates (politically improbable), earnings can rise only
with continued prosperity, and their growth has been decelerating for a couple of years even as stocks passed 9000 and
10,000 on the Dow Industrials. Thus, a case could be made
in early 1999 that a perfect scenario is required to remain in
place to prevent any market decline. That sort of situation is
the equivalent of a useful cautionary question (about individual stocks or the general market): "How can the news get
any better?" Aside from possibly cautionary implications for
1999, this discussion highlights the importance of always
knowing your assumptions and being able to name those
which the market seems to be already using. Changes in
assumptions cause major changes in price level!

RISING INFLATION IS USUALLY A KILLER, BUT IT IS NOT REQUIRED

Rising inflation drives bond interest rates to rise (whether
forced by the Federal Reserve Board (FRB) or freely determined in the long-term bond market). High bond yields put
stocks on the defensive. Until the middle 1960s, when the
markets became fixated on rising inflation in the Vietnam
conflict period, bond and stock prices traditionally moved as
if on a seesaw. An expanding economy drove earnings and
thus stocks' prices higher until overheating occurred. Rates
began rising, hurting bonds and eventually putting a clamp
on business expansion. Then came a recession, cutting earnings and stock prices, but bolstering bond prices, as yields
fell due to light borrowing demand. Finally, cheap money
encouraged businesses to resume investment for expansion,
and the next boom began, eventually leading to overheating.
And so on and so on.

Until about mid-1997, stock investors hung on every twist
in any indicator that seemed to forecast inflation. What was
bad for bonds became bad for stocks at the same time, so the
two markets ran in tandem nearly constantly for about 30

years. Since mid-1997, perhaps the fear of resurgent inflation has begun being buried: for whatever reason, stocks' sensitivity to bond yields has decreased.

Are we going back to the older, seesaw-type pattern? One cannot be sure. But one can envision two major scenarios, which imply radically different types of safe havens when stocks are due to correct.

> *Scenario #1.*   Stocks to decline because of weak economic conditions (domestic or worldwide), implying lower corporate earnings and slack demand for lending.
>
> *Scenario #2.*   Stocks to decline because of rising inflation or serious FRB efforts to raise interest rates. May or may not imply a recession, but does forecast higher bond yields.

In scenario #1, repositioning some of your money from stocks into high-quality bonds is a smart move. Slackening business implies declining interest rates, which will create higher bond prices and attractive total returns (including price appreciation) in bonds. But in scenario #2, higher interest rates imply declines in bond as well as stock prices. Therefore, in that scenario, money market funds are the only refuge (unless you see runaway inflation, in which case gold will have a rare sustained upward move).

In scenario #2, your patience will be sorely tested: you will want to "do something"; staying out of both stocks and bonds will make you itchy for action. Try to remember that it's not necessary to be fully invested at all times. Sometimes cash, although providing a low return, is better than losing money in other asset classes. Within your equity allocation, the same applies: it is not always necessary to buy something just because you've sold a stock or a mutual fund. Equities don't go up every day or every month!

In summary, advanced stock prices cannot survive in the face of rising or high interest rates, which are usually driven by rising inflation. But those conditions are not required for a bear market in stocks to start. The other ways a bear market can start include declines in corporate earnings, expectations of declining earnings, or simply the existence of historically high valuation measures following a speculative run-up. When expectations are extremely optimistic, it can take only a tiny disappointment to undermine the love-in chemistry between investors and their stock and fund holdings.

A VOTE AGAINST CDs

Should you run for the extremely safe-feeling cover of CDs when you pull out of stocks? Never! CDs lock in your money, imposing at least an actual dollar cost to escape when you should go back to stocks, and probably also a psychological lock-in mentality (penalty avoidance) that will keep you in the CD too long. If long-term CD rates are high and therefore the most tempting, you can be sure that bond rates will be high as well (recall 1980–1981?). You'll be afraid of stocks because of their recent response to gravity, and will be tempted to "lock in today's high rates" on a CD. Well, if your timing is anywhere near right, say within a year or so, you will be much better to buy long-term *bonds* now and stocks soon after, since the inevitable recession will prick the up cycle in rates, first rallying bonds and then cheering stocks as economic recovery starts to appear.

Locking in high rates should be done in bonds and long-term bond funds, not CDs, because the former can be liquidated instantly for better opportunities in stocks or for a move back to money market funds if a renewed rise in interest rates seems pending. Because of their immediate and convenient liquidity, money market funds are always a better tactical choice than even a very short CD: your options are always psychologically and financially more open outside the CD environment.

GENERAL STOCK MARKET HIGHS USUALLY FEATURE ROUNDING TOPS

Most cyclical tops in stock markets come in the form of a rounding-over pattern rather than a sharp final spike. A spike would require some surprising and hugely bullish news, or else not all stocks could be driven higher at once from already lofty levels following two or more years of rising averages. (Remember from Table 2-2 that bull markets are about 70 percent likely to run two or three years rather than more or less than that.) Most often, a market tops out in a pattern of rotating and generally narrowing leadership. One industry, sector cluster, or concept group after another will have a terrific last-gasp rally and then will start to rest. Speculators and momentum followers will move elsewhere, to whatever areas of the market are still hot or seem cheap, and those in turn will have their last hurrahs. Sooner or later, previously leading groups will be tried out for another run, but if failing to make new highs they will quickly be abandoned and start to move lower again.

Cumulatively, fewer groups and individual stocks will still be going up. You will feel some rising personal frustration, as the popular averages still seem to be rising while your diversified portfolio seems stuck in neutral. You should watch carefully in *Barron's* and *The Wall Street Journal* for mentions of "narrowing leadership," as this is a sign of a tired market in which increasingly fewer stocks are rising smartly and thus holding up the "averages" somewhat artificially. When the last heroes peak out, there will be no leaders left, and the race for the exits will become a stampede.

How can you mathematically track this repeating phenomenon? If you utilize a major database such as Metastock or Value Line or AAII's Stock Selector, you can track breadth of leadership. Experience teaches that examining net price changes over a nine-month (or 39-week) window is a good indicator—neither too slow nor too sensitive to every weekly jiggle. You may need to download the data onto a spreadsheet and calculate and then rank percentage changes, because major databases focus on weekly, monthly, or 12-month changes. Tracking the percentage of stocks currently showing nine-month gains is referred to as using a "diffusion indicator."

Midway to a little past midway (timewise) in a bull market, the percent of nine-month winners will be around 90 percent. When it starts to decline, the latter days are present! Once it reaches, and definitely when it falls below, 50 percent, the bull market has rounded its top and prices will surely head down. You should never hope against hope that a bounce from 50 percent will happen: positive psychology has been routed and a full-blown cleanout in the form of a panic sell-off will be required before new highs in the averages can be seen again.

In summary, tops in the general market occur when, taken as a whole, conditions can't really get any better. Corporate earnings have risen for quite a while, expectations remain high (meaning almost any surprise will be disappointing rather than positive), and the psychology of participants is buoyant. A few pieces of bad news will not be backbreaking immediately. But you will begin to notice that good news does not drive new price gains the way it had in past quarters. That's a sign of a "tired market" or one where such high expectations are already built into prices that things basically have little or no room to get any better.

Unsuccessful investors (and traders) always perceive risk incorrectly. (Being wrong means feeling no risk at a top, and being mortally frightened at a bottom!) At the time a market is making its major top, you will be anything but frightened. There will still be plenty of good economic statistics to take comfort from. At least one highly visible industry group (in early 1999, both Internet and oil stocks) will be rallying, making you and others feel confident. You will therefore feel no urgency to move to the sidelines. You will actually feel lonely if you do so, because all those around you will be celebrating their recent successes and anticipating that prices will be going higher still. Psychological hint: A top is defined by the absence of any more players willing or able to bet more money that things will get even better. General market tops are formed gradually rather than suddenly. By definition, tops always occur in times of great confidence!

No two tops are the same, no matter what angle one tries to measure them from. As apologists like to repeat to give themselves extended hope, it truly is always "different this time"—in the details. But if you step back and look at the big picture, many (but not literally all) patterns repeat as market tops are being created.

Observable Quantitative Signs of High/Risky Stock Markets

- Two years or longer with no correction of at least 10 percent in the major averages.
- Two years with consecutive percentage gains in the high teens or greater.
- One year with a gain in the upper 20 percents or more.
- Generally strong corporate news, widely expected to persist.
- A long period of economic expansion already in place.
- Existence of low interest rates and the pervasive assumption they will continue.
- Big percentage gains in low-priced and small- to medium-capitalization stocks, outrunning gains in the major averages.
- A wild speculative fad in at least one investment theme or industry group (Internet stocks in 1998–1999).
- Large numbers of new companies going public.
- Enormous (multi-hundred percent) immediate gains in hot initial public offerings' prices.

- Very strong net dollar inflows into stock mutual funds (published one full calendar month late by the Investment Company Institute and about two weeks sooner by Lipper Inc.).
- Financial services stocks among the leading market groups.
- Numerous huge corporate mergers, typically entirely financed with stock rather than cash as the currency.

Prevailing Behavioral and Emotional Attitudes Signaling Tops

- A general "don't-worry-be-happy" response to any expressions of caution or dissent.
- Expectations of historically incorrectly high returns from stocks.
- Unusual numbers of young people (and also older first-time investors) joining the party.
- Mocking and public derision of anyone expressing minority views.
- Declarations that the newest technology has created "a whole new paradigm" in which all past standards should be considered irrelevant.
- Pronouncements that "it's different this time." At the detail level, it always will be! But by the time market supporters need to clutch at straws to declare old standards outmoded, the advance is so extended that it needs such stretches of reasoning for its own justification.
- Frequent general magazine coverage of the bull market's wonders and presumed continued rosy prospects.
- Stock market exploits are an everyday topic of conversation at the office, the club, parties, and in TV sitcoms and late-night monologues.

- Local newspapers carry gleeful headlines about the bull market. (This story is not their primary business; the very fact they are fixated on stocks tells you the advance has been all-consuming!)

- Magazine stories of ordinary couples who have become millionaires and are able to retire unexpectedly early.

- Your personal feeling that you've gotten pretty savvy about investing and/or that your assets have grown handsomely enough that you might consider early retirement.

- People quitting their jobs to manage their investments; day trading brokerage offices springing up in major cities.

- Increasing use of leverage without fear of its downside.

- Discovery, invention, or implementation of some new financial strategy or instrument that seemingly promises major profits with apparently no risk (e.g., program trading in the late 1980s and derivatives in the mid-1990s).

- Popular enshrinement of financial gurus as folk heroes. Examples are revered brokerage strategists/prognosti-cators and, recently, very hot mutual fund portfolio managers. Such winners take time to emerge and seem proven; that time itself requires an aging bull phase.

Personal Warning Signs to Beware

- Virtually all of your stocks show paper gains. (To check this one, you must first ignore those stubbornly held old dogs that have been longtime snoozers and have no realistic hope of recovery; check the rest!)

- You're spending more time during breaks at work and/or at home on evenings and weekends checking the market on the Internet or doing library research for new ideas.

- You buy and sell more frequently than in the past, and often trade for quick gains.

- You're not horrified at the thought of using margin or options to leverage your returns—techniques you rejected a couple of years earlier in a lower market.

- You perceive little or no risk.

- You find yourself counting your chips more often than in the past (doing so is fun only when stocks are high!).

HOW TO IDENTIFY A TOP IN REAL TIME

Anyone can look at a chart of past market movements and point to a top. To win the contest by protecting your capital, you must be able to identify a high and topping market while it is happening, not several months later! This is an art, not a science. But that should not deter you from being observant and keeping some checklists. Because we live in a newsbite age, we're overwhelmed by too much information with too little context and by too little integration of the daily fragments. If only there were a certain magic number of critical factors that would signal a market top. Sorry, there is not! Market tops are characterized by clusterings of such phenomena. The very first few will not be the last or only ones. I'd encourage you to photocopy the lists of conditions just provided, and then make notations of actual happenings (and their dates) during each bull-market cycle. When you have a fairly large collection of scribblings in the margin, sell some stocks. Don't wait for 100 percent completion of conditions on the list! No two markets are exactly alike, nor will they all include every item listed. Look for a preponderance of the evidence, as a jury would.

EXPECT CYCLES TO REMAIN SHORTER THAN IN THE PAST

If forced to guess, I would predict that bull-market cycles will be shorter and tops more frequent than in the past: more two-year or shorter runs and fewer that extend to four years without a 10+ percent correction. I would bet on sharper price moves, both up and down. Why is this so, and what does it imply for investors' actions?

The world of information is one of electronic speed. Living without the Internet is virtually the equivalent of dwelling under a rock! Everyone else has information at Net speed, and many act on it. People react quickly because they expect most other participants to do so, and they do not want to be late getting in or out. Pushing the "send order" button on a PC is easier to do than talking through an idea (to buy or to sell) with a broker. Paid money managers are forced— by too-frequent benchmarking of their performance—to join this herd mentality. They feel they virtually must own the hot-momentum names, and when the slightest thing goes wrong they can exercise no patience. Value is an intolerably long-term concept, because price performance *right now* is king.

Whether you like it or not, this mentality appears unlikely to unwind. By implication, then, you should expect high volatility and shorter rather than longer-lasting trends. Prices will get out of sync with realistic value, either to the upside or the downside, relatively quickly. Price moves measured as percents per month will be faster, in both directions. Therefore, you must lean toward greater activity than in the past, lest you overstay.* This looks like one of those regrettable situations where you can't beat the crowd so the only winning approach is to join it. However, joining the crowd *late* is always a losing approach. To win, you must move in the opposite direction of the long-prevailing trend before the stampede starts and everyone else has already moved prices sharply toward their next turning point. Fortunately, general markets tend to round over rather than spike. That gives you a little time to act. But not as much as in the past. It is better

---

*For example, major Internet discount brokerage stocks doubled in seven days and then fell 50 percent in five days during April 1999!

and emotionally easier to sell before the top than after it. And those are the only available, realistic choices; you will catch an exact top only with 100 percent blind luck.

SUMMARY

This chapter has focused on identifying and taking responsive action to developing tops in the overall stock market. Chapter 4 will provide you with 50 years' history and pictures of actual market tops. Then, Chapter 5 will zero in on patterns in individual stocks, which perhaps surprisingly are considerably different—especially in the age of the Internet! If you learn to identify and take advantage of signs of tops in individual stocks, cumulatively by that process you will take care of reducing your equity exposure while the general market is forming its rounding top with narrowing leadership. Whichever approach you take can work: top-down (spying the rounding top) or bottom-up (selling individual stocks that peak). But you must practice at least one of them, or else you'll be condemned to wasting time and money riding through the next down cycle that erases much of the gains of the past two or more years. Stay on your toes!

4

HALF A CENTURY'S HISTORY OF ACTUAL MARKET TOPS

C HAPTER 3 DISCUSSED AND documented the frequency and general characteristics of stock market topping phases. We now turn to actual history to review events, conditions, and even the pictorial details (via charts) of past tops, through and including that which preceded the scary 20 percent smash in the summer of 1998. Our intention is not to write comprehensive historical accounts of each cycle, as has been done at great length concerning the 1920s and the 1929 crash. Rather, we will capsulize the natures of multiple recent historical high markets—half a century's worth—in a consistently formatted treatment. This approach allows easy comparison and contrast across episodes and enables the reader to digest many years' facts in a manageable package size.

APPROACH

For each of the market top phases from 1950 through 1998, we will provide the following:

- A chart showing the shape and length of the topping phase
- Description of basic shape or type of market top
- Length of rising phase, in months
- Length of subsequent declining phase, in months
- Percentage gain in bull phase and slope, expressed in percent per month
- Percentage decline and slope, in percent per month, of subsequent bear market
- Percentage of bull gains wiped out or taken back by following decline
- Length of time required for market to equal again its prior high
- Brief characterization of "hot" investment concepts or industries leading the bull phase
- Identification of triggering negative(s) cited as responsible for ending the bull market

While each market student may place differing values on these various perspectives of the historical material presented, the final four listed should be especially of interest and personal use. Declines are almost universally measured in major-average points or, more properly, percentages. As a practical matter, however, that scale is somewhat arbitrary and sterile. First, the average individual investor's equity portfolio almost always loses a greater percentage than the major averages, mainly because it typically contains some companies in deepening trouble and also because it usually involves at least some high-volatility stocks rather than all blue-chip giants. Second, and more personally, market declines wipe out gains and take precious time to be recouped afterward. Those aspects are more vivid to an individual investor than is the specific percentage decline of some chosen major market average. They are also personally meaningful even for those rare investors who religiously hold only an index fund based on the S&P 500.

The final two critical factors listed illustrate the French idiom that the more things change, the more they seem the same. One is struck by the wide variety of different industries, new investment concepts, and emerging technologies that dominated late-stage bull markets from one cycle to the next. Literally, such would support the claims of those who say shortly before each market top that "it's different this time." In the details, of course. In broad concept, however, one of a very short list of patterns recurs. Credit explosion, an exciting new technology/industry, and/or some new financial instrument appears. The late 1990s saw the Internet on center stage, "changing our lives"—as had the telegraph, transcontinental railroads, radio, the horseless carriage, and contraceptive pills in earlier times.

Triggering causes are also interesting, and more often than not have differed from one market or economic cycle to another. In most cases, some unexpected external factor upsets the happy applecart; occasionally a known but presumed-containable problem (e.g., a local war) balloons to frightening and seemingly unmanageable proportions. Often, the process of forming a market top is gradual; in other cases, stocks turn lower on a dime overnight. One must be prepared and watchful for both possibilities after any lengthy upswing (three or more years). I believe you should factor into your investment strategy and tactics an expectation that the new era of electronic trading and instantaneous worldwide information/opinion/rumor dissemination—both lacking any emotional buffering or enforced waiting before taking action—implies more violent and probably more frequent declines than in the past. Volatility appears unlikely to do us the kindness of retreating. All of this implies a heightened need to be ready to take prompt action to defend your assets. Putting that more positively: taking profits when they are presented is both a pleasant and prudent exercise, for one cannot know when adversity will return.

That said, let us proceed to examine actual tops of markets in recent decades.* Bear in mind a clear underlying message that market tops are far from rare events and therefore cannot prudently be wished away if you want to build wealth at an above-average rate for a lifetime.

THE FIFTIES

The first decade following World War II saw two significant market tops, spaced not atypically: more than three years apart. The first, in January 1953, followed over three years of rising prices at what by current standards seems a moderate pace: 1.9 percent per month. The top in 1956 followed a shorter but sharper bull market which saw the Dow Jones Industrial Average (DJIA) gain 104 percent in 30 months. This was followed by a rather gradual decline lasting 18 months and taking away 19 percent of the major average, but also wiping out nearly 40 percent of the prior bull market. That decline was no doubt elongated by a recession's appearance.

THE SIXTIES

The 1960s, which historians cite as a time when America lost its innocence, were not a very happy time for investors. Four significant tops occurred—in 1960, 1961, 1966, and 1968. Two of the four subsequent declines each wiped out more than the entire preceding bull market had bestowed in terms of gains. As history now shows, a great inflation was born in 1965 with the guns-*and*-butter policy of the Johnson administration; rising inflation and interest rates proved lethal for both stock and bond investors.

*Historical charts of Dow Jones Industrial Average courtesy of Securities Research Co., Wellesley, MA, (781) 235-0900.

Final top: January 1953

Shape of top: Rounding

Longevity and height of rise:
43 months; 81.8%

Slope of rise: 1.90% per month

Longevity of decline: 8.5
months

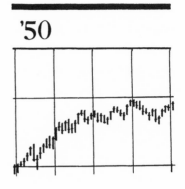

Percent size and slope of
decline: 13%; 1.53% per
month

Percent of bull erased: 29%

Time to regain old top: 14 months

Hot industry, concept: Capital goods, housing, metals

Decline trigger(s): Fears of postwar recession, which did
begin late 1953

Final top: April 1956

Shape of top: Rounding

Longevity and height of rise: 30.5 months; 103.9%

Slope of rise: 3.41% per month

Longevity of decline: 18.5 months

Percent size and slope of
decline: 19.4%; 1.05% per
month

Percent of bull erased: 38%

Time to regain old top: 28
months

Hot industry, concept: Steel,
autos, consumer goods

Decline trigger(s): Fears of
recession, which did occur
starting late 1957

Final top: January 1960

Shape of top: Rounding

Longevity and height of rise:
    26.5 months; 63.3%

Slope of rise: 2.39% per month

Longevity of decline: 10
    months

Percent size and slope of
    decline: 17.4%; 1.74% per
    month

Percent of bull erased: 49%

Time to regain old top: 15 months

Hot industry, concept: Defense, capital goods, autos

Decline trigger(s): Recession

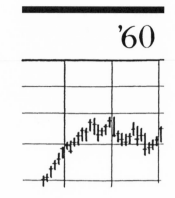

Final top: November 1961

Shape of top: Rounding

Longevity and height of rise: 13.5 months; 29.8%

Slope of rise: 2.21% per month

Longevity of decline: 6.5 months

Percent size and slope of decline:
    27.1%; 4.17% per month

Percent of bull erased: 118% (!)

Time to regain old top: 21
    months

Hot industry, concept: Electron-
    ics, defense

Decline trigger(s): Cuban ten-
    sions; later JFK versus steel
    industry showdown

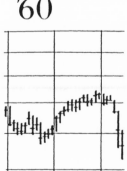

Final top: February 1966

Shape of top: No sign; inverted V

Longevity and height of rise: 44 months; 32.4%

Slope of rise: 0.74% per month

Longevity of decline: 8 months

Percent size and slope of decline: 25.2%; 3.15% per month

Percent of bull erased: 55%

Time to regain old top: 82 months (!)

Hot industry, concept: Electronics, birth control, defense, airlines

Decline trigger(s): Dislocations due to Vietnam conflict

'65

Final top: December 1968

Shape of top: Decelerating, rounding

Longevity and height of rise: 8.5 months; 21.6%

Slope of rise: 2.54% per month

Longevity of decline: 17.5 months

Percent size and slope of decline: 36.7%; 2.10 percent per month

Percent of bull erased: 210% (!!)

Time to regain old top: 47 months

Hot industry, concept: Defense, aerospace

Decline trigger(s): Recession induced by LBJ's 10% income tax surcharge

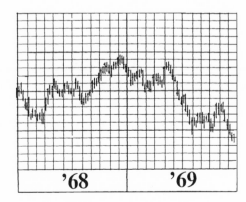

'68   '69

THE SEVENTIES

The 1970s saw three major stock market tops, in 1971, 1973, and 1976. These followed short bull markets, none of which extended to even 24 months. The decline of 1973–1974 is referred to by brokers and money managers who endured it as a constant daily water torture. The net slope of that decline was only 2 percent per month, but its 24 months seemed to extend interminably. Conditions were made dreary by the pinch on purchasing power induced by OPEC's oil-price rise, which touched off sharper inflation. The decline following the 1976 high was the most gradual in the half century, at only 0.65 percent per month, but it extended to 29 percent in total. It took over six years for stocks to reach a new all-time high again. The long, painful process of inflation cast its dark shadow throughout the decade.

Final top: April 1971

Shape of top: No sign; inverted V

Longevity and height of rise: 11 months; 51.8%

Slope of rise: 4.71% per month

Longevity of decline: 7 months

Percent size and slope of decline:
    17.2%; 2.45% per month

Percent of bull erased: 50%

Time to regain old top: 11.5
    months

Hot industry, concept: Defense,
    electronics

Decline trigger(s): Malaise over
    Vietnam War length, inflation

'71

Final top: January 1973

Shape of top: Rounding, after
sharp prior rise

Longevity and height of rise: 12.5
months; 34.9%

Slope of rise: 2.79% per month

Longevity of decline: 23 months

Percent size and slope of decline:
46.6% (!); 2.02% per month

Percent of bull erased: 180% (!)

Time to regain old top: 118
months (!!)

Hot industry, concept: Consumer electronics, airlines

Decline trigger(s): Inflation; Watergate; worsened by
OPEC embargo and sharp recession

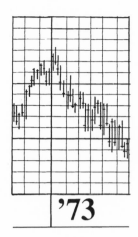

Final top: September 1976

Shape of top: Rounding

Longevity and height of rise: 21.5 months; 80%

Slope of rise: 3.72% per month

Longevity of decline: 45 months

Percent size and slope of decline:
29.1% (0.65% per month)

Percent of bull erased: 66%

Time to regain old top: 73
months (!)

Hot industry, concept: Energy;
conservation; environmental
quality

Decline trigger(s): Stagflation—
drag of OPEC-induced
inflation

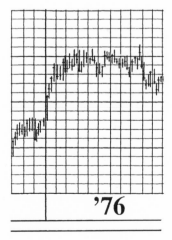

THE EIGHTIES

By the end of the 1980s, investors began benefiting from the historically pivotal economic policies of lower taxation and inflation busting introduced by President Reagan. Before that financially happy conclusion, however, four more market tops would be seen, namely, those in 1981, 1983, 1989— and one cannot forget the assumptions-undoing "big one," the crash of 1987.

Curiously, each decline following a major top was shorter than the one before it: from slightly over 15 months in 1981 to under two weeks of fury in October 1989. Extending to a full 6.5 months, the decline following the 1983 top still stands as twice as long in time as any that investors have endured since then: a generation of investors has learned ever since 1987 that "you buy the dips because they never last." *Never* is a very long word for real historians.

Final top: April 1981

Shape of top: Rounding

Longevity and height of rise: 13 months; 41.4%

Slope of rise: 3.18% per month

Longevity of decline: 15.5 months

Percent size and slope of decline: 25%; 1.61% per month

Percent of bull erased: 95%

Time to regain old top: 18 months

Hot industry, concept: Resources; inflation hedges; gold; real estate

Decline trigger(s): Recession induced by tight credit designed to rein in inflation

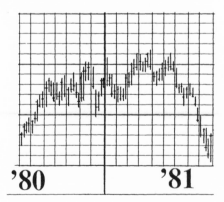

'80   '81

Final top: November 1983

Shape of top: Rounding

Longevity and height of
    rise: 15.5 months;
    67.8%

Slope of rise: 4.38% per
    month

Longevity of decline: 6.5
    months

Percent size and slope of
    decline: 16.8%; 2.59%
    per month

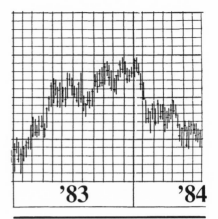

Percent of bull erased: 42%

Time to regain old top: 14 months

Hot industry, concept: Takeovers; biotechnology, pharma-
    ceuticals

Decline trigger(s): AT&T breakup; AIDS virus labeled
    worldwide crisis

Final top: August 1987

Shape of top: Narrowed leadership; acceleration/blowoff

Longevity and height of rise: 23
    months; 155.3%

Slope of rise: 6.75% per month

Longevity of decline: 2.5 months

Percent size and slope of decline:
    41.2%; 16.5% per month (!!)

Percent of bull erased: 68%

Time to regain old top: 24 months

Hot industry, concept: Exporters,
    mergers, IPOs

Decline trigger(s): Rising interest
    rates

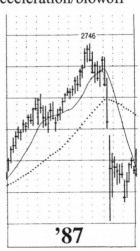

Final top: October 1989

Shape of top: No sign; inverted **V**

Longevity and height of rise:
   23.5 months; 73.8%

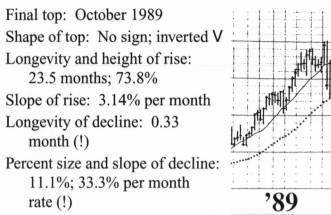

Slope of rise: 3.14% per month

Longevity of decline: 0.33
   month (!)

Percent size and slope of decline:
   11.1%; 33.3% per month
   rate (!)

Percent of bull erased: 26%

Time to regain old top: 7 months

Hot industry, concept: Megamergers financed by junk-
   bond leverage

Decline trigger(s): Psychological reminders of October 1987
   and fears of liquidity squeeze; junk-bond market collapse

Final top: July 1990

Shape of top: No sign; inverted **V**

Longevity and height of rise: 9 months; 21.1%

Slope of rise: 2.35% per month

Longevity of decline: 3 months

Percent size and slope of decline: 22.5%; 7.5% per month

Percent of bull erased:
   129% (!)

Time to regain old top: 10.5
   months

Hot industry, concept: Gam-
   ing stocks

Decline trigger(s): Banking,
   S&L crisis; liquidity fears;
   rising energy costs; prep
   for Gulf War

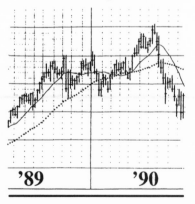

Final top: February 1994

Shape of top: No sign; inverted V

Longevity and height of rise: 40 months; 70.6%

Slope of rise: 1.77% per month

Longevity of decline: 2 months

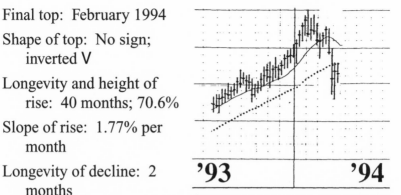

'93   '94

Percent size and slope of decline: 11%; 5.5% per month

Percent of bull erased: 27%

Time to regain old top: 13 months

Hot industry, concept: International; exporting; capital goods; technology industries

Decline trigger(s): "Tequila effect" following Mexican peso flotation; sharply rising U.S. interest rates

Final top: July 1998

Shape of top: Rounded

Longevity and height of rise: 42 months; 162.9%

Slope of rise: 3.88% per month

Longevity of decline: 2.5 months

Percent size and slope of decline: 20.9%; 8.37% per month

Percent of bull erased: 8.4% (small!)

Time to regain old top: 4 months

Hot industry, concept: Financial services; Internet, e-commerce

Decline trigger(s): Credit defaults and sharp recessions in Russia, Asia, Latin America

'97   '98

THE NINETIES

The final decade of the old century was generally characterized not only by an unprecedented net run-up resulting in
historically unprecedented average compounded gains in the
upper teens per year, but these recent years were also marked
by several notably short but also very sharp declines. One
might suspect, but cannot prove, that the cult of momentum-
chasing, near-term-performance-greedy money managers,
augmented by the speed of trading over the Internet and the
ease of fund swapping through supermarkets were factors
changing the typical shape of both up and down cycles.

Another interesting pattern that might cause lost sleep is
that the prolonged (nearly unprecedented) domestic economic expansion in the United States was not enough to prevent three or four fairly nasty market episodes in the past
decade. All were triggered by overseas events: preparation
for and dislocations from the Gulf War, and three bouts of
unrest due to overseas defaults, devaluations, and recessions
(Mexico in 1984, emerging Asian nations in 1997, and Russia in 1998). No nation is an island!

In any event, stocks declined after a top in 1990,
retreated grudgingly and only mildly in 1994 under the
weight of rising interest rates, and suffered sharp corrections
following run-ups in 1997 and 1998 (these pages were written in early 1999, so history may hold yet another episode
before 2000). Interestingly, in this decade three tops returned
to the old historical pattern of coming four years apart. As
this was written, some market commentators were fearing a
decline just before the year 2000, perhaps induced by possible economic dislocations due to the Y2K bug.

OBSERVATIONS

While market lore has it that October and May and, to an
extent, February are the bad months in the stock market
(months in which large and often climactic declines occur),
it is interesting to note that only two of the 16 market *tops*

chronicled in this chapter occurred in any of those months. And the top in October 1989 preceded a vicious decline lasting only 10 days. It might be well for investors to take note that a suspicious 7 of the 16 market tops took place in the months between December and February. Thus, it turns out that the environmentally or externally "dangerous" markets—meaning high ones—occurred in the wintry months. The "internally" perilous times, when careful management of one's own emotions is critical, are in May and October. Then the danger lies not in high prices but in losing nerve at just the wrong time and selling rather than buying in low markets! It is a general truism that investors collectively always perceive danger, or the lack thereof, incorrectly— we're fearless in high markets and terrified at bottoms!

The relative slopes of the bull markets that led to the tops, and of the bear markets that followed, display an intriguing and perhaps ominous pattern. Prior to 1987, in only 2 of the 11 cases were the declines sharper in percent per month than the preceding advances had been. Starting in 1987, all five of the declines were more violent in character. These later bear markets have also been extremely short by historical standards, averaging just over two months' longevity. We have been somewhat spoiled since August 1982: bull markets have been short, and our emotional staying power has been tested only on the price dimension rather than also on a time-endurance basis. How will we feel in some future market decline if it extends over 45 months, as did the 1976–1980 decline, or over 23 months as in 1973–1974? "Just in case" is yet another valid argument for pruning the ripened fruit when market advances extend to three years or more.

In sum, the last half of the twentieth century produced no fewer than 16 significant market tops—again emphasizing that one per three years is a fairly realistic expectation. This again would be a reason to lighten equity commitments after about a 36-month rise in stocks. Likewise, as a signal that caution is always healthy, many of the tops since 1987 have been of the inverted-V shape, while the large majority of those in the prior decades had been rounded or more gradual in shape—affording some advance notice. In recent years, the predominant characteristic of high markets has been narrowed leadership; popular big-cap averages such as the Dow Jones Industrials and the Standard & Poor's 500 have far outrun the broader list of stocks and then suddenly joined the others in a sharp downturn.

5

TOPS IN INDIVIDUAL STOCKS

N CHAPTERS 3 AND 4, we explored typical characteristics and the actual history of general market tops. Knowing these is important, so you can identify times when stocks are getting set to reduce your wealth—unless you take action. Here, we will examine how individual stocks form their tops. What's quite interesting is a considerable difference in patterns: usually, the broad market creates a rounded top with narrowing leadership, but more often than not individual stocks make sharp price peaks. It turns out that a number of factors help identify which stocks are peak-prone. It is also helpful that certain telltale signs readily identify peaks exactly as they are being made.

BACKGROUND AND ASSUMPTIONS

We must begin this discussion with several key statements and assumptions. These are necessary to enunciate as anti-

dotes to the widespread cultural bias in favor of holding forever, which we consider to be a passive victim's strategy—
one destined to create actual results that are average at best.
So let us state our stipulations and premises:

- Granted, in the long run stocks of good companies will
  go higher on a net basis.

- However, history has repeatedly demonstrated that in
  the interim, stocks' prices move from excesses on the
  high side to excesses on the low side.

- Even stocks of great companies and clear leaders in
  their industries can be at significant price risk from
  time to time.

- Unacceptably major price breaks in a company's stock
  do not even require earnings declines, general bear
  markets, or a recession.

- Because of advances in worldwide commerce and
  accelerations in technological change, no company
  should be considered permanently immune to assault
  and possible conquest.

- You do not need to hold even great companies' stocks
  every week or even every year, because sometimes they
  are too risky (high).

- No market action (buying or selling) should be felt to
  be forever—taken permanently or irreversibly.

The foregoing points outline our case for your need to be
agile rather than ruled by inertia. Chapter 6 will delve into
technical analysis for identifying tops. Chapter 7 will cover
the necessary psychological preparation for action (particularly to pull the selling trigger). But for the present, let us
look at the evidence on how individual stocks sometimes
carry excessive capital risk and how they tend to act while
forming price tops.

EVEN GREAT STOCKS GET HIGH AND PUT YOUR CAPITAL AT RISK

In the long term, stocks' values are determined by fundamentals such as earnings, dividends, cash flows, assets, and prevailing economic conditions and interest rates. But on the road to the long term, stock prices are set daily by supply and demand representing the actions of buyers and sellers making investment (and speculative) decisions. Psychology surrounding industry groups and individual stocks recurringly moves from one great extreme to another. It does not take a decline in earnings, a general bear market, or even a recession to cause even a leading company's stock to drop—often by a huge percentage.

Table 5-1 chronicles stunning price declines in industry-leading companies' stocks in recent years. What is most significant is that nearly all these stocks suffered such horrendous price markdowns in years when the overall stock market was not in net decline! Only a few of the 18 stocks listed in Table 5-1 represent high-technology situations. (That is a particularly volatile portion of the equity markets, as will be discussed later.)

Stock prices often move to extremes on expectations, and sometimes the climate of expectations takes on a life of its own. Professional money managers in many cases pursue momentum-chasing strategies, in which they hold (or buy more) shares that are performing most extraordinarily—and this can lead to significant relative overvaluation. Sometimes the slightest change in expectations is all that's required to break the positive psychology for a stock or group. For example, in the summer of 1996, Intel advised analysts that its June quarter's earnings would rise "only" 30 percent rather than the 35 percent widely projected. Its stock dropped 26 points in two hours on record trading volume.

When you hold individual stocks that have performed heroically, you must realize that you are at increasingly large wealth risk the further their prices rise. If stock prices rose in

TABLE 5-1   Major declines in industry-leading companies' stocks

Stock	Industry	Percent drop	Period
Genentech	Biotech	78	1987–1988
Compaq	Computers	70	1991
Xerox	Office equipment	66	1987–1990*
Halliburton	Energy services	63	1990–1992
Circus Circus	Gaming	60	1993–1994
Southwest Airlines	Airline	60	1994
BankAmerica	Banking	59	1985–1986
Tiffany & Co.	Luxury retail	57	1992
Safeway	Groceries	55	1991–1992
IBM	Computers	54	1992
Winn-Dixie	Groceries	54	1993–1994
British Petroleum	Int'l oil	53	1990–1992
Kroger	Groceries	53	1991–1992
First Mississippi	Fertilizer	52	1992
AMR Corp.	Airline	51	1989
Bristol-Myers	Drugs	44	1992–1994
Sara Lee	Foods, etc.	42	1991–1993
Johnson & Johnson	Health care	39	1992–1993

*Slight net decline in DJIA.

direct parallel with earnings, and no more, there would be little problem in holding a McDonald's or a Johnson & Johnson forever. Market reality, however, is that stock prices fluctuate much more widely than company fortunes—and this is due to the momentum of rising expectations. During 1997, excluding closed-end funds and stocks trading under $5, common stocks on the New York Stock Exchange (NYSE) generated approximately an 11 percent rise in EPS, but their stock prices averaged a percentage range of over 60 percent!

When price is running sharply ahead of fundamentals, P/E levels are becoming historically too high, and psychology toward the stock in question is becoming unsustainably optimistic. Whether you think in terms of a fundamental or an emotional viewpoint, at some point the stock cannot continue going up. (And with momentum as a guiding rule for so many portfolio managers, there *will* be a rush to the exits once the advance stops.)

Unless you're willing to suffer a potentially sickening decline in price (and thereby expose your capital to the added risk that you will finally sell in panic regrettably close to the exact bottom), you must take action to sell individual stocks that have treated you extremely well over relatively short periods (one to three years, or in some extreme cases, just a few months). It will always be difficult to sell such stocks, because you will be maximally infatuated with them (and with your own brilliance) at just the time they are most grossly overpriced! While Chapter 7 will work on developing a more rational and introspective mind-set, here we will focus on objectively identifying factors disposing stocks to peaky price behavior.

MOST STOCKS PEAK RATHER THAN ROUND OVER

It might seem contradictory to note that major market averages often make rounded tops while industry groups and individual stocks more often than not stage sharp and accelerating rallies that form price peaks. Remember that major market averages are designed to represent wide diversification across industries and thus reflect "the market" broadly. Therefore they include stocks from a spectrum of industry groups. Not all industry groups or individual stocks move in lockstep; they very typically make their own tops at different times. For example, in the great bull market of 1997–1998, these groups (among others) made highs as follows:

Real estate investment trusts (REITs) in September 1997

Autos, natural gas, and oil in October

Energy services in December

Biotech, foods, transportation, chemicals, and utilities
in March 1998

Precious metals, defense, brokerage, and broadcasting
in April

Papers, forest products, environmental, and natural gas
in May

Airlines in June

Telecom, housing, leisure, regional banks, computers,
health care, retailing, and software in July

While "the market" as measured by the DJIA topped out
on July 17 of 1998 at over 9300 before declining about 2000
points, quite a number of industries and individual stocks
had seen their highs well before summer. Two very useful
barometers that reveal the inner breadth of market strength
are numbers of new highs and the cumulative advance-
decline line. These are graphed for 1997–1998 in Figures
5-1 and 5-2. The advance-decline line (although it has some

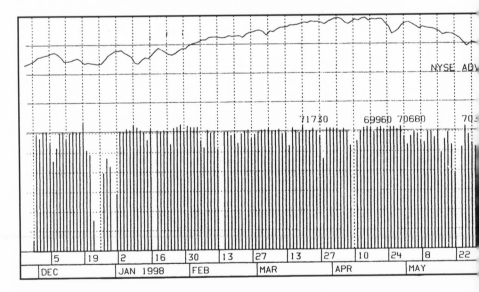

FIGURE 5-1   Twelve-month NYSE cumulative daily advance-decline line.
Chart courtesy of Daily Graphs, P.O. Box 66919, Los Angeles, CA 90066,
(800) 472-7479; www.dailygraphs.com.

problems due to inclusion of many hundreds of preferred stocks, utilities, and closed-end bond funds among NYSE listings) is simply a running total of daily net differences of advances less declines. What its graph shows, in absolutely historically classic fashion, is a persistent deterioration of net advances while price "averages" continue rising, led by fewer and fewer individual sharp risers.

Changes in opinion, often crystallized by news developments, move stock prices. When opinion has been favorable for some time (many months or longer, typically), fewer nonbelievers still exist. Many investors are already on board and are in love. Good news under such circumstances can readily cause a *brief and sharp acceleration in price gains*. The few nonholders jump on board at last; the few traders who have sold short panic and cover; and existing holders are feeling righteous and have no inclination to sell out on great news. There is a radical although temporary imbalance between supply of and demand for shares in the affected company or group.

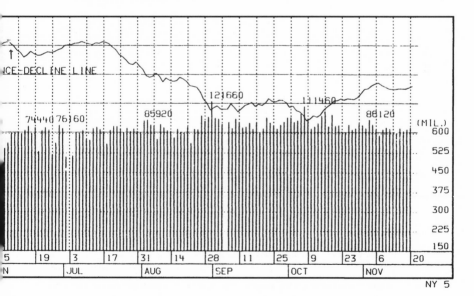

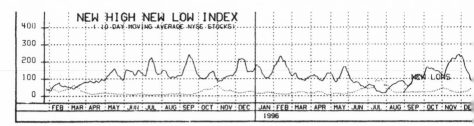

FIGURE 5-2   New highs and new lows, NYSE, 1995–1998.
Chart courtesy of Daily Graphs, P.O. Box 66919, Los Angeles, CA 90066,
(800) 472-7479; www.dailygraphs.com.

Examples of such accelerations are illustrated in the
graphs in Figures 5-3 to 5-7. September 1997 saw a temporary craze for REITs as investors sought yield and perceived
value; energy-services stocks shot up in October and November as major consolidating mergers were announced; utility
stocks soared in March 1998 when interest rates declined;
telecom and Internet stocks rocketed in an amazing craze in
June and July; biotechnology stocks accelerated in July on
news of some breakthroughs against cancer and AIDS.

**FIGURE 5-3   Two-year daily chart of Fidelity Equity Income Fund Real
Estate Investment Portfolio.**
Chart courtesy of http://www.BigCharts.com.

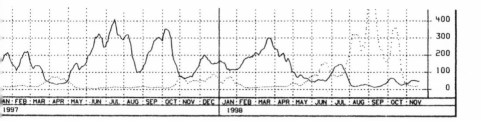

FACTORS DISPOSING STOCKS AND GROUPS TO PEAKY PRICE PATTERNS

Some stocks seem more prone to sharp price peaks, while others (the relative minority) tend to top out less dramatically. Peaking behavior seems to be conditioned by certain characteristics of companies or industries, while a list of event drivers can also be compiled. Factors disposing a stock (or its industry group) to peaky rather than rounded price tops fall into two broad categories (see Table 5-2 on page 66).

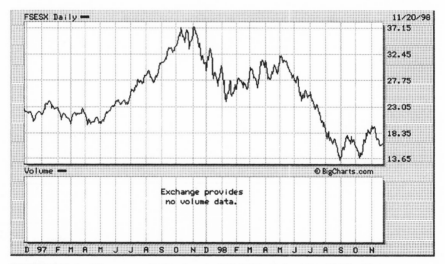

FIGURE 5-4   Two-year daily chart of Fidelity Select Portfolios Energy Services Portfolio.
Chart courtesy of http://www.BigCharts.com.

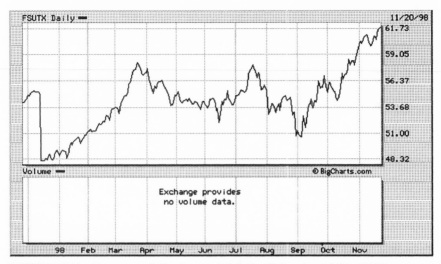

FIGURE 5-5   One-year daily chart of Fidelity Select Portfolios Utility Portfolio.
Chart courtesy of http://www.BigCharts.com.

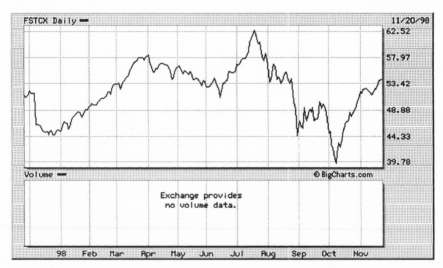

FIGURE 5-6   One-year daily chart of Fidelity Select Portfolios Telecommunications Portfolio.
Chart courtesy of http://www.BigCharts.com.

FIGURE 5-7   One-year daily chart of Fidelity Select Portfolios Biotechnology Portfolio.
Chart courtesy of http://www.BigCharts.com.

By contrast, as a broad generalization, very mature cyclical companies, huge companies, those offering high yields, and those broadly held by individuals tend to trade in less volatile or spiky patterns. Likewise, companies that frequently release current operating statistics (retailers, restaurants, auto manufacturers) hold relatively low potential for extremely positive surprises and therefore tend to trade back and forth rather than going on streaks.

Some highlights and examples from Table 5-2 are instructive. A sharp conceptual identity about a company or an industry makes the shares especially subject to concentrated buying or selling action in response to either news or a clear change in opinion. For example, FDX (formerly Federal Express) forms a precise mental picture about its business: it delivers packages for business, and it is sensitive to economic changes and cost of fuel. Halliburton services the oil industry, and its revenues are sensitive to drilling activity, in turn driven by price changes in oil. In late 1998, Amazon.com became a focus

TABLE 5-2   Characteristics disposing stocks to peaky price tops

Company/Industry Factors	Stock-Related Factors
Sharp conceptual identity	Low institutional holdings
High technology	Large insiders/low float
One of few pure plays	Small or micro-cap
Highly economically sensitive	Thinly traded
Fashion, trendy or single-product	Low or zero yield
Leveraged capitalization	Large short position
High growth/high expectations	Relatively recent IPOs
Zero, or very high, exporting	Light brokerage coverage
Blockbuster news potential	
Infrequent news dissemination	

stock for the concept of commerce on the Internet. Chase Manhattan and J. P. Morgan are immediately thought of in connection with international lending. Charles Schwab and Merrill Lynch respond sensitively to changes in public sentiment toward the stock market. If there is a positive event or change in a key factor (inflation, raw materials prices, etc.), and you can easily name a company that should benefit, you have a stock that will be peaky (and will tend to dive on any clearly bad news). For example, if oil prices decline, buy American Airlines (AMR); if oil prices rise, buy British Petroleum/ Amoco.

Some other examples will illustrate concepts in the left-hand column. A company with heavy debt is more sensitive to changes in revenue than companies with less leverage. Thus, for example, Stone Container reacts more sharply to economic expansion than Union Camp. Puerto Rican Cement is an obvious pure play on repairs and reconstruction after hurricanes on the island; Fedders comes to mind instantly when a widespread heat wave grips the nation. Toy manufacturers and ladies' fashion makers are subject to hot new items catching on (or not!). Lone Star Steakhouse would be thought a big winner if the prices of beef dropped; so would Ben & Jerry's if butterfat costs retreated.

The factors in the right-hand column refer to characteristics of the stock itself (rather than the company) that tend to lead to light supply and demand, which in turn can foster peaky price patterns. Suffice it to say that this type of knife cuts both ways: when there is bad news, or if micro-cap stocks go out of favor, price plunges can be very deep.

KEY EVENTS ACT AS (CONTRARIAN) SELLING SIGNALS

Positive events crystallize news coverage and thereby strongly affect investor perceptions. The age of Internet communications, on-line newspaper summaries, full-session financial TV coverage networks, and high institutional momentum sensitivity is here. You should expect rapid and substantial price change in response to news. Press releases are now disseminated on the Internet rather than by mail. Netscape and AOL announced their merger on the Net (of course!) in November 1998. There are few secrets that travel slowly now that The Motley Fool and other Internet chat rooms spread the word worldwide in just minutes. These factors, by concentrating the impact of news and changing psychological disposition toward a stock, heighten the stakes. Stocks rise further ever faster and thereby become overpriced in less time than in the past. When all the buyers are satisfied and momentum stops rising, the fast-money players exit for the next game and the price rise unravels. The stock market never was very forgiving, but now it has become merciless. One can apply the description "love-hate relationship" to investors and stocks. Except these days there are fewer investors and many traders!

Given this acute market sensitivity to events, you need a list of major drivers likely to create rapid price acceleration. (See Table 5-3.) Play out the scenario in your mind. Then you will realize fairly quickly that all the activated buyers have been satisfied in a burst of high-volume buying that shoots prices skyward. And then what? Literally, there is no available answer to the question, "How could the news get any better here, so that opinion could become even more rosy than it is right now?" Big price gains, on huge volume, triggered by news that "everyone" now knows, briefly spells profit-capturing opportunity but at the same time extremely high capital risk for the lazy long-term holder. The stock is up in the air and has nowhere to go but down in the medium term! It is important in such circumstances to act very promptly, because extreme mass emotional reactions to discrete news now play out in a matter of mere days.

TABLE 5-3   Focused event drivers for stock price blowoffs

Macroeconomic Picture

Big currency changes affecting exports/imports

Significant interest rate declines

War and peace

Cartel pricing moves or failures

Agricultural/weather-pattern changes

Changes in world economic assumptions

Major political control shift

Tax changes

Company-Specific Events

Takeovers in the industry

Deregulation

Regulation or law requiring company product or service

Awarding of major contracts

Signing of strategic-alliance agreements

Investment by a major company

Significant scientific breakthrough

Stock-Related Items

Stock entering S&P 500 or Russell 2000

Filing of 13-D by high-profile investor(s)

Major analyst's strong "buy" advice

Aggressive stock buyback despite high price

Partial tender or Dutch auction

You will find it a useful perspective to remember that the news might be great for the company or industry, *but* that does not mean the stock will continue going straight up from today's already elevated level forever. Great companies' stocks decline as well as rise. When they get ahead of themselves, you certainly will not catch the exact top by selling. But if you stay around, you will experience a prolonged period of emotional unwinding before a new assault on the old, high prices can occur. Temporary maximum good news literally must be topped, or the price has seen its best already. Mentally test whether you may be observing a maximum collective emotional reaction to news, impacting prices unsustainably.

What factors can you use to judge, in the heat of the daily trading and rapid price movement, that "this is it"?

- External environment
    - Major news that everyone, including non-investors, discusses
    - Sometimes, a boost from nonfinancial TV coverage
    - Postweekend final burst of support
    - Quarter-end window dressing
- Observable stock-trading evidence
    - Multiple-day upsurge followed by a lower-volume day
    - Unusually large excess of latest price over 10-week moving average
    - Extremely heavy trading volume

In the sense of maximum possible favorable news and attention as just described, major news being widely discussed beyond narrow investor circles is a sure sign of a price top very close at hand. Probably the most memorable recent example was the explosion of media coverage, talk-show banter, water-cooler whispering, and late-night humor about Viagra, Pfizer's male potency aid that gained FDA approval in the spring of 1998. As shown in Figure 5-8, that company's stock jumped roughly 30 percent in a matter of weeks and peaked out on huge trading volume after a crescendo of trading lasting about a week. The best news came when press reports circulated that 40,000 new prescriptions were being written weekly. For investors, the price run-up was very pleasant but also presented a dilemma: the price could not hold when judged in psychological terms, so even with those enhanced longer-term profit prospects the drug brought, stepping aside to buy back later was the clear choice. Not only could the news not possibly get any better, but the logical sequence called for it to get worse: there might be adverse side effects (heart attacks); there could be (and were) major insurers limiting or denying reimbursement on "recreational use" grounds; and eventually the pace of new customers would be reported as slowing. Even with a great new drug, one did not need to take the risk of owning the stock every single day or week.

Sometimes TV coverage (which now has broader effect than print media) can create a surge of positive interest in a stock. Major news-magazine shows might feature an antiburglary gadget deterring auto thefts, or an existing drug now accidentally found to have positive effects for a second medical condition. Private-prison stories, PC software for learning, and new endorsements by major athletes or other nationally recognized personalities usually have a notable effect on producing companies' stocks. Features on the Beanie Babies craze boosted McDonald's, and news that all the teenagers "simply must own" a certain brand of sneakers or boom box have similar effect on the producers' and retailers' shares. Fads pass, and memory of a single network news show is even shorter. Sell on the news—into the excitement!

One often-useful pattern, especially when a bull market is boiling along with plenty of public participation, is the

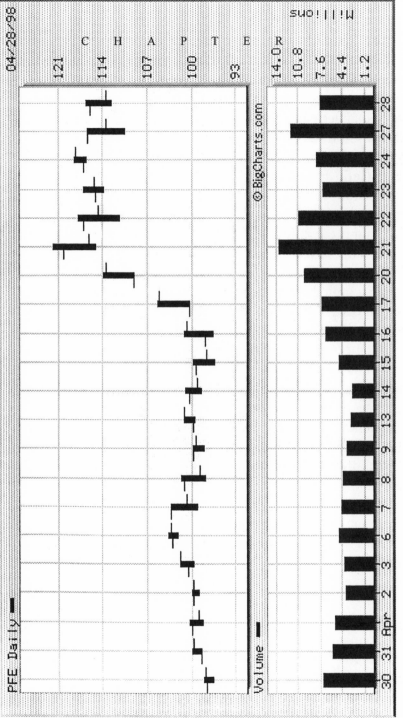

FIGURE 5-8 **Illustration of volume and price crescendos driven by news: One-month daily chart of Pfizer Inc.** *Chart courtesy of http://www.BigCharts.com.*

71

postweekend last gasp. Some company has been in the news and its stock has risen smartly during the past week. Over the weekend, weekend-warrior-type investors marvel at the big price jump in the Sunday newspaper, read the accompanying story or check out the cause via the Internet, and buy on Monday. Tuesday morning pretty much rounds up any late-comers to the party, and the game is over. This pattern can be very useful in helping you set micro-selling tactics. If you see it, you can wait until late Monday or into Tuesday after the opening, or you can mentally project a little further price gain and place a limit selling order above market and let the stock come to you and take you out pleasantly. The latter tactic frees you from watching constantly and also prevents your becoming more greedy and proud and infatuated as the price moves higher—and from holding on past the end of the near-term game.

At the ends of calendar quarters, and especially at the end of December, stocks having recently performed very well are not current candidates for selling by portfolio managers—until right after the quarter closes. This is called *window dressing*—the practice of painting the most favorable-looking picture possible for those who will examine portfolio holdings (retirement plan trustees or mutual fund shareholders and directors). Stocks that have been great performers are not for sale until the calendar page turns. That creates a temporary lack of supply, meaning that normal demand will force price upward in a spurt. The calendar tells you when the game will end. Use that information to your advantage!

VOLUME CRESCENDOS

Observing the pattern of trading in excellent-news dramas can usually provide wonderful selling clues if you are watching for the investor psychology that changing price and volume data reveal. A classic peaking-out pattern is one where a given stock rises for three to six days in a row, with heavier trading volume each session. Think about that: volume is the market's blood pressure on display. Sooner or later, all who will be excited to action have joined the game, and the intensity of media coverage starts waning. At that time, trading volume no longer will expand. After a price has risen for several consecutive days, higher volume becomes required, with two implications. First, more volume tells you there are still more people just coming into the stock than in previous days. Second, and very important, rising buying volume starts becoming required in order to accommodate the shorter-term and perhaps nervous holders who begin wanting to take their profits. Big buying is needed because there are lots of them; a fade in demand means the price cannot be held up any longer. My repeated experience is that four to five days of a volume crescendo with strongly rising price is about the limit you should ever hope for. Beyond that, you are on borrowed time and will see shrinking capital. Sell. You can always buy back later!

One other excellent way of telling when a stock's price has gotten too far ahead of itself (literally) is to note the positive divergence between current price and the 10-week moving average. (See Figure 5-9.) Each stock has its own personality and its own pattern of volatility in price moves. Popular charting packages on major quote-vendors' services and several free Internet charting packages allow a plot of the moving average to be overlaid on a price chart. Look at the stock over the past couple of years and note the size of the gaps between daily price and the then-current moving average for each time that stock made temporary peaks.

When you see a similar price advantage in real time, sell the stock despite its current popularity and good news. The vertical size of the space between price and moving average is a measure of upside extremity or exhaustion. Describing it in a different way, the momentum that the stock has already enjoyed is so extreme that it cannot be sustained or exceeded. The higher a stock goes in short order, the more

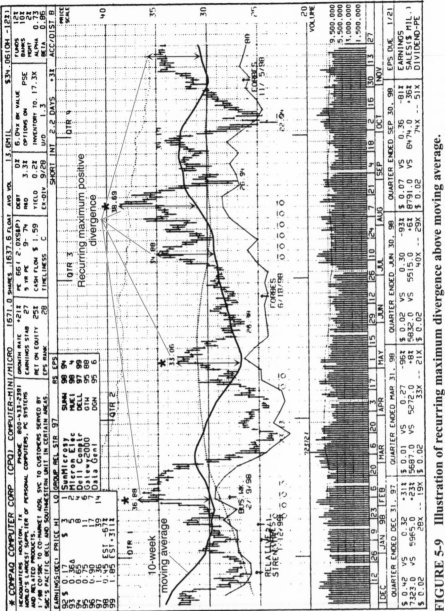

FIGURE 5-9 Illustration of recurring maximum divergence above moving average.

Chart courtesy of Daily Graphs, P.O. Box 66919, Los Angeles, CA 90066, (800) 472-7479; www.dailygraphs.com.

potential profit takers are activated. Their selling will cascade as soon as the advance slows. Increasingly widespread use of computerized monitoring of stocks means that lots of players are easily monitoring such patterns and will jump when they see extremes developing in line with past norms. We live in an age when everything in life has been speeded up; it is unavoidable. Prompt action is required. Remember, tens of thousands of investors are watching the Internet, their fingers poised over the "transmit order" key, intently tracking the stock you also own.

One final and very valuable item must be observed. As noted, trading volume is more than just a number; it literally measures the frenzy of investor activity in a stock. Here the Internet provides an instantaneous means of checking history, whether you look during a trading session or before tomorrow morning's opening. Extremely heavy volume usually signals the immediate or virtually imminent end of a price trend (up or down!). Why? Maximum trading volume and rapid price change compared with historical norms tells you opinion has become more violently unbalanced than ever before. That imbalance cannot be sustained or topped.

If you note that a stock has risen on volume that's its highest or even second highest in a year or longer, you have an extremely valid measure of highly unusual emotional behavior. The price will turn around in a matter of hours. I have reviewed thousands of charts and have found that high volume in a 12-month period almost without exception coincides with a meaningful price high or low. If the stock has risen on extremely high volume, you know the extreme will not prove to be a price low! If you doubt this, take an hour to thumb through *Daily Graphs* at the local public library or brokerage office branch. That will convince you. Then you will need same-day awareness for executing actual orders, so on-line charting will be required for optimum execution.

TWO TECHNICAL ANALYSIS POINTS

Stock prices do not move randomly or in a vacuum. Supply and demand for a company's stock are the causes, and price change is the effect. Not always does price (and volume) activity tell a clear story, but sometimes loud bells are being rung. One such bell ringer was just discussed. Another is what technical analysts call a one-day reversal on heavy volume, which occurs at significant turning points in price, both tops and bottoms. Here we focus on *tops*—reversals where price has been rising but then turns down, with heavy trading involved. Whatever has caused this pattern to occur (midday news, a technical price target reached, an analyst reversing opinion or lowering EPS estimates, etc.), it is meaningful in the marketplace. A lot of people were buying and suddenly the tide was reversed and a lot of people decided to sell (some recent buyers included!). That marks a turning point of opinion in the minds of a large number of market participants. You may not personally be a big believer in technical analysis, but its proper use does reflect changing psychology observed in the market. And changes in perception and expectations are what cause changed behavior. A heavy-volume one-day reversal from up to down is an urgent signal to take your money off the table. Don't look back wistfully in hopes that top will soon be revisited.

Another technical analysis observation that reveals investor psychology is the closing of a previous downside gap. Suppose that a stock was trading at a relatively high price for some period of time and then it experienced a sudden gap to the downside in price. Maybe overnight the company issued surprisingly bad earnings news, or its chemical plant blew up, or the FDA disapproved its wonder drug, or some other reason(s) caused an avalanche of selling that made the stock open a lot lower than it had closed. That downside move will have some ongoing momentum as more investors hear the news, some trailing stop-loss orders are triggered into market sells, and other holders either become panicky or (in extreme cases) receive margin calls. The stock will move a considerable distance down from its pre-gap price until ready sellers are exhausted and some bargain hunters gain courage.

Now carefully consider the mental state of those who have held on through that carnage. Collectively, they are thinking, "Gosh [or maybe *&#$&@!], I wish I'd sold that thing before disaster struck. Mark my words: if it *ever* gets back up to $X a share, I'll take my money and run!" And you know what? They do exactly that. In the Glaxo chart (Figure 5-10) the magic number was $62. After the first shock, when the passage of time, psychological recovery, and some bargain hunting finally brought the price up to its pre-gap level, sellers came out of the woodwork (and off the specialists' book page) in large numbers, and the price could not hold its gains. If you have a stock that fills a gap, take your profit (or your repaired loss) and stand aside for the next supply/demand cycle to play out. You will be reducing risk and can virtually bank on buying back that stock later for less.

CONCLUDING OBSERVATIONS ON THE SALE OF INDIVIDUAL STOCKS

Selling a stock that's up is always difficult to do. You will be infatuated and proud and will enjoy the companionship of your attractive friend. Remember that doing what is uncomfortable rather than obvious works best in investing (buying in panics and selling during general jubilation). When your stock is up, you will be sure it will go higher and will want to cling to it for the proverbial last eighth. That's a losing bet: you will never be that lucky or that perfectly skillful. Take your big recent gain and let someone else risk owning it for the final few percents.

After having observed one or several of the price-peaking patterns described in this chapter, if you are still hesitant about selling immediately when their signals are

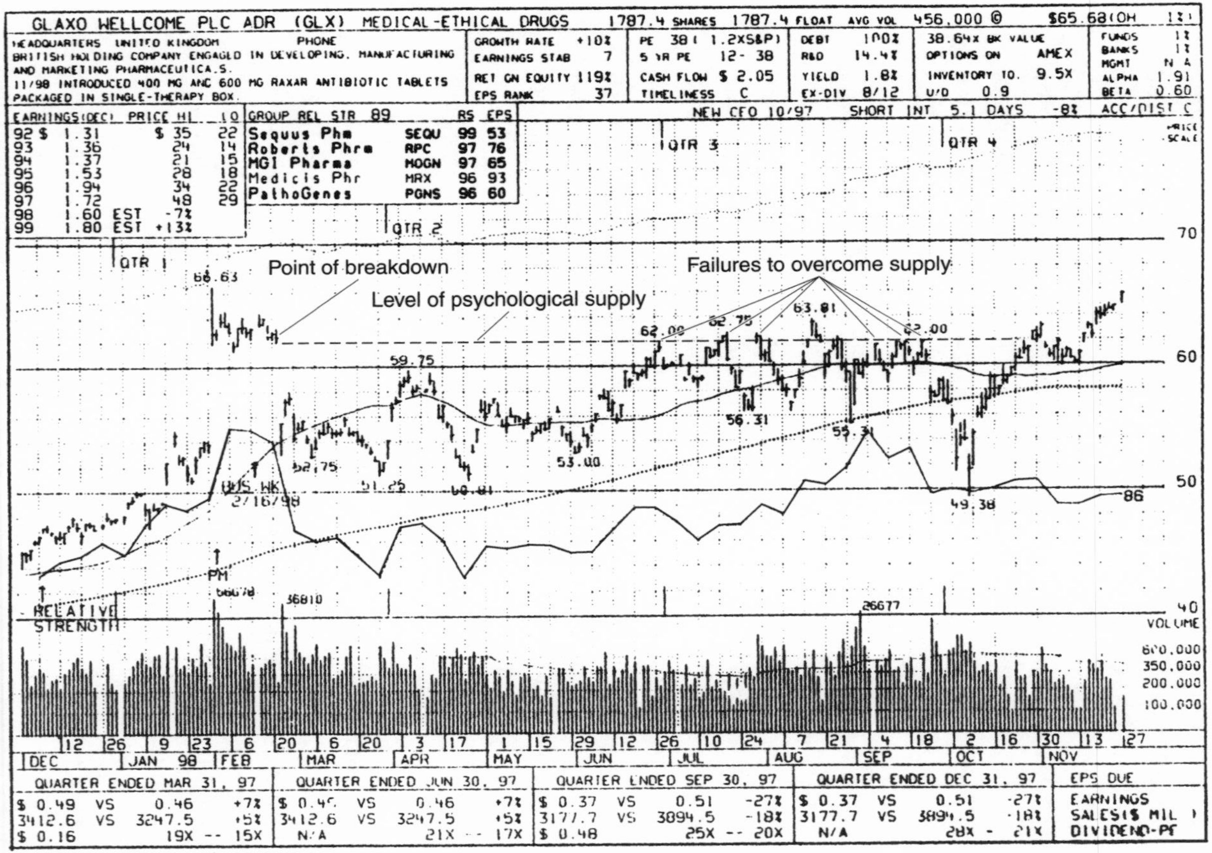

FIGURE 5-10 Illustration of lingering effects of downside price gap.
*Chart courtesy of Daily Graphs, P.O. Box 66919, Los Angeles, CA 90066, (800) 472-7479;
www.dailygraphs.com.*

being flashed, ask yourself a critical question: "Would I *buy* this stock right now at this advanced price?"

What you would not buy right now ("Well, it really is somewhat ahead of itself," or "Gosh, that P/E is historically a little rich for my blood") you should not hold. Read the following words twice or more and let them sink in: holding is passive, commission-free buying.

Holding commits your capital anew for tomorrow exactly where you had it yesterday and today. Holding should be an active choice, not a default. Making a choice proactively is all the more critical when your stock is far extended on the upside (fundamentally or technically, with or without the benefit of recent good news or general market buoyancy). When stocks are high, more of your chips are on the table and subject to confiscation.

Finally, getting accustomed to selling is a good exercise because it loosens up your market reflexes and thereby allows you to be more nimble the next time action is warranted. Winning (taking a good but unreasonably large profit and/or avoiding a price downturn by having sold) will also provide very positive feedback in your investment head, helping you to act with more self-confidence in the future.

And selling stocks that have enjoyed outrageous recent success just plain cuts your risk of giving back your hard-won gains. Waste not, want not.

6

TECHNICAL ANALYSIS: TOOL FOR IDENTIFYING TOPS IN STOCKS

U NLESS YOU ARE THE truly rare investor who holds only an index fund, you will need to know how to identify tops that form in individual stocks. The object is to get out closer to, and before, major tops rather than near frightening subsequent bottoms. This chapter does not presume to provide a complete education in technical analysis.

Here, in summary, we wish to alert you to both price patterns and (the considerably less studied) trading-volume patterns that typify top areas in individual stocks. Knowing these, you should be more ready to sell out your holdings on a timely basis if they start acting suspiciously. As a number of your individual stocks do so one after another, you will both identify a general market pattern of topping out and in the process will exercise the discipline to reduce your equity exposure in an orderly way in preparation for the coming decline.

This author believes that technical analysis is every bit as important as the conventionally more revered fundamentals in determining profits and losses in the stock market. Over my four decades of market study and active participation, I have concluded that technical analysis (1) works, and (2) works *because* that approach to market tracking and measurement by nature reflects the very real and changing collective psychological state of investors. Perceptions and stimuli produce decisions to take buying and selling actions, which in turn move prices. One can know the market by understanding the players in it. Those who hold passively do not change prices; those who exercise decisions do, and their collective crowd behavior defines momentum and its reversals.

PRICE PATTERNS

The following characterizations of 9 major types of action that precede tops include not only physical or shape descriptions, but also a related analysis of the psychological or emotional shifts taking place that are played out on the chartist's page.

CHANNEL BREAKS

A price channel is a series of higher highs and higher lows in a stock's price history, in which the lows can be connected by a clearly defined line and the highs by another (usually parallel) well-defined straight line. The successively rising highs and lows in turn reflect short-term ebbs and flows of enchantment with the stock. Nothing goes up every day. In terms of momentum, the slope of a channel indicates the net difference in urgency or persistence of demand over supply (rising channel) or vice versa. Enough investors and traders watch chart patterns so that the breakdown of price below the lower trendline is an event causing considerable selling. Critics say that technicians thus create the action that they predict in what becomes a self-fulfilling prophecy. Whatever causes the stock price history to cease rising in the previously orderly and defined channel, one must concede that something has changed in the mental landscape. Whether it be softening fundamental expectations or some emotional hesitation toward the stock, a new phase has begun when a channel breaks.

Two resolutions can follow a channel break. Sometimes the stock goes immediately into a prolonged and large-percentage decline. In other cases, particularly if the overall market is still moving higher, an individual stock can shift into a lower gear, defining a new channel with a lesser upward tilt. Seldom will more than two breaks be followed by flatter-sloping new channels. By then, any possible lesser slope would be flat or downward. Also, the sharper the original angle of slope, the less likely a slower angle is than a meaningful correction first. This is because wildly rising prices rapidly create overvaluation and also attract aggressive traders who, in droves and in each other's footsteps, will abandon a stock at its first sign of slowing momentum.

TRIANGLE BREAKDOWNS

A triangle depicts a period of time in which the battle between buyers and sellers becomes more highly pitched in intensity within an ever narrowing range of prices. First the bulls and then the bears take a run, only to be held at bay and turned back. In rising markets, two types of triangles are most common. One has a flat price top and rising bottoms, forming a rising wedge. Here, sellers in considerable numbers will repeatedly disgorge shares at the same price (flat top). Usually, they are eventually satisfied, and such a triangle is resolved upward to a new high. A second bull-market triangle has declining tops as well as rising bottoms, in effect forming a rightward-narrowing pennant. In psychological terms, this means that buyers and sellers are evenly matched and take brief turns dominating the trend. But all the while they are becoming more tightly clustered and fervent in their opinion about the proper price. The resolution or "breakout" typically takes not more than 80 percent of the time from left wall to projected point, and is usually violent in the direction of the winning side.

A third type of triangle has a more ominous implication. This one has a flat bottom (or sometimes a mildly downward-sloping bottom), but its top consists of successive rises that fail to reach earlier highs. This declining triangle or declining wedge nearly always ends in a downturn. In psychological terms, the bulls are able to support the stock repeatedly at the same low price level; however, their ability to drive it higher against the bears' selling diminishes with each later thrust. That can be because the bulls are running lower on enthusiasm or due to an increasingly large camp of sellers ready to unload on any rally. Either explanation clearly has negative implications for the future. Declining triangles are strong sell signs; the best one can do is get out near one of the successively weaker rises delineated by a downward-sloping top line.

WIDENING SPRINGS

A widening spring, or coil-shaped formation, is relatively rare. From left to right it has the opposite direction of the banner shape described earlier. Each move, both up and down, is wider than the ones before it. This sequence of price changes reflects increasingly violent emotional and perceptual behavior by those actively trading in the stock. On the whole, investors dislike volatility. Usually, a coil is resolved to the downside, as participants can no longer push each rise for even more points to make a higher high—and the psychological underpinnings of the stock break down. Usually, the decline is violent.

ROUNDING TOPS

A rounding top is like an inverted saucer, and more often than not it is fairly gradual or flattish rather than sharply curved in shape. This formation is not as neatly defined by ruler's edge as is a series of sequentially flatter-sloped channels. But the psychological underpinnings are quite similar. The stock continues rising, but it is both mathematically and emotionally decelerating. It is rising (probably carried by general market momentum and buoyancy), but it is losing steam. This shape reflects a very gradual but cumulatively important shift in an increasing number of investors' opinions about the stock. Buyers are required if a stock is to rise. When the army of interested parties loses its urgency or enthusiasm and gradually drifts off to pursue other interests, the balance of power shifts toward sellers, who then have more chance of turning the curve down when some negative market or company event intrudes. A rounding top gives holders time to stage a graceful exit. But once it has rounded over, a long time will be needed before a new high is attainable. The collective opinion will be like a large ocean liner that takes considerable time to turn a full 180° in either direction. Often, rounding tops characterize huge companies' stocks rather than tiny firms' prices—probably because the population of participants is so large in the former case and therefore its on-balance or net mood changes only gradually.

HEAD-AND-SHOULDERS TOPS

A head and shoulders is somewhat like a rounding top in terms of the shifting opinion and relative strengths of the camps holding that opinion. It is not quite as smooth in terms of curvature on the upper side. As the description implies, one can see three tops, the second of which is highest, with the other two at nearly an equal but lower price level. The second, or right-hand, shoulder, once it forms, signifies that buyers have failed to move the stock to another new high as they formerly could or wished to. Future weakness is implied. Precise technicians believe that the subsequent decline will be of as many points again as the distance from the top of the head to the neckline, which was the level at which the declines on each side of the head were stopped. That's a lot of points.

Psychologically, a head and shoulders is a powerful and clearly visible display that the stock's enthusiasts have lost their nerve or their numerical supremacy. The second shoulder itself usually represents a breakdown from a previously rising channel or slope—itself an early warning of trouble ahead. After a head is formed, tight trailing stops should be placed under the price as the potential right shoulder rises. They will not be touched if the stock is to resume a rise to new heights, but will give you a much better exit point than if you wait and react after the breakdown clearly occurs and then sell at market.

DOWNSIDE PRICE GAP LATER FILLED

Price gaps, whether upside or downside, almost always occur in response to some significant news occurring between trading sessions. A large number of shareholders are motivated, all at the same time, to sell their stock at market; this causes a considerable price concession easily visible on the stock's price chart and is always accompanied by very high trading volume. When a downside price gap occurs, its existence sets up a later situation in which the stock will very predictably find large supply at such future time as it returns to its prebreakdown price level. Investors seeking to lighten their equity positions should use the closing of a previous gap as an immediate signal to sell their shares at market. One such chart (of Glaxo) was shown in Chapter 5; more detailed analysis is provided here.

Why does the downside gap's closing have the effect described? Once again, we find a technical analysis formation underpinned by logical understanding of collective emotional responses from investors. Suppose a stock is trading along fairly routinely and closes one day at $48. Before the next opening bell, important negative news is released:

FDA drug approval denied, shockingly lower earnings, or whatever. Our stock opens the next morning, perhaps even with a little time delay due to the huge imbalance of orders, at $41, down $7. Over the next several days these shares trade in a range between perhaps 38 and 42, as investors digest the news and decide what to do at the newly established price level.

What is going on in the heads of holders who owned the stock at $48 before its gap? They are thinking, "Mark my words, when that dog ever gets back to 48, I'm going to sell like I should have before the bad news!" Never mind that these folks had no real way of foreseeing impending bad news. In their heads they wish they'd sold at 48, so they have now set up 48 as their target price. When our stock finally regains some followers and returns in time to 48, a large number of sellers are waiting as if in ambush, ready to end its price rally. "Aha," they all exhale, "finally I've got my chance to get even." And they sell. Buyers may still like the company, but for some reason invisible to them their further bids just do not seem to push the price higher. An army of sellers is holding the line at or just below or just above 48. Seeing that for some reason the 48 area represents a stall point for the shares, traders back off, pulling their buy orders and, in some cases, joining the selling out of frustration. They want their cash for use in some other stock that's still moving.

This shift in balance from buyers to sellers turns back the price. The stock may gradually fall several points, perhaps to 44 or 45, before bargain seekers attempt another rally. Once again, it is likely that 48 will become a supply zone, as investors who did not follow their prior resolve to exit if it ever reached 48 now keep their promises and get out. More supply, and a repeat performance of a price ceiling. Technical analysts see a double top formed at 48, and they, too, pull out. And down goes the quote again. Thus, the price level that existed just prior to the downside gap becomes an important supply zone and one at which savvy investors sell rather than hope for a rally.

The longer the stock had traded around or above its pre-break price level, the more numerous the regretful older holders who are "just waiting," and therefore the greater the difficulty the stock will have in piercing its pre-break level. On the other side, if a very long time (perhaps several years) passes before any first return to (in our example) 48, memories will have been dulled, many holders will have given up and sold lower in frustration or for tax losses, and that pre-break level may not uncover as much stock for sale as it would in a only few weeks or months. In a generally but not wildly rising market, psychology surrounding a downside gap being closed is especially strong: people are no longer in love with the stock that's hurt them but instead are now eager to "get out even" and use their money in other promising stocks they see passing them by. This dynamic sets up a powerful case for not holding in hope of an unlikely move past the pre-break price level.

VOLUME PATTERNS
Thus far, we have described and emotionally characterized *price* formations, which are the most commonly watched material of technicians. I believe that volume is a critical and very telling element as well. The following three volume patterns, when they accompany certain price formations, signal trouble ahead and should be cause for very prompt selling. While the thrust of this book is to guide investors through a lifetime approach to investing rather than to convert them into short-term traders, volume patterns such as those subsequently described do in fact play out in a matter of days rather than months or quarters. Therefore, being responsive to them represents an attempt at fine-tuning shorter-term timing of what should be strategic moves. In other words, if a bull phase has extended for a long time and/or your equity representation is well above its appropriate percentage level, the

appearance of ominous short-term volume (or price) patterns can act as a trigger for taking necessary action promptly and will in the process produce favorable exit points in highly vulnerable individual stocks.

VOLUME FADES

Equilibrium between buyers and sellers in a given stock means that prices move very little, with small upward and downward fluctuations during a day mainly reflecting the imperfectly matched timing of individual orders reaching the trading floor—or the emotional influence of the general market moving significantly in one direction. A persistent imbalance of orders, reflecting a predominance of either sellers or buyers, naturally causes net movement in price— what some technicians would call an *uptrend* (or *down-trend*). When the crowd of people who want to buy has finally been satisfied, they are no longer present with buy orders, and a different balance against the number of sellers is established.

Buyers acting mainly on rational or fundamental grounds may back away, because at some point the new (higher) price level no longer seems attractive to them. Or, in a more emotionally dominated atmosphere, those stimulated by some company/industry news or media event, or even by rapid price change itself, play out their impulses and collectively are transformed from would-be buyers to actual new holders. Whether the driver for buying be fundamental (rational) or emotional, when it has been satisfied in a large portion of the would-be actors, there is no longer a net balance of eager buyers present and able to push price still higher. When price rises for several days, or even on balance over a period of a few weeks, on gradually decreasing trading volume, a clear sign is being given that total demand is becoming less urgent and less large.

Stock prices can decline of their own weight (lack of buyers in the face of even relatively normal selling activity).

But prices cannot rise without the pressure of active buyers—those who express demand for a stock in sufficient quantity that they must bid up the price in order to find enough willing sellers. It takes buying to push up prices. When the number of buyers dwindles, rising price cannot be sustained. Trading volume is an instant and constantly visible barometer of pressure. A combination of high volume and rising price is bullish, reflecting strong and active interest, as indicated in Figure 6-1. Rising price on dwindling or low volume is bearish, saying that although the enthusiasts still have the upper hand their numbers are fading.

Therefore a *volume fade*—a series of days during which price rises while volume decreases—is a sign that the advance will soon be finished. The buyers are approaching satiation and their numbers are waning. Prompt selling is implied, and will reward those investors and traders alert enough to note this pattern of activity.

VOLUME CRESCENDOS

In what may seem a strange or even contradictory irony, a sharp *crescendo* of trading volume also signals the nearby end of a price trend (whether that price move be upward or downward).

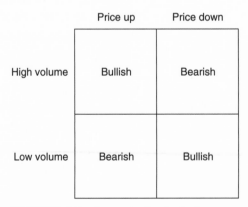

FIGURE 6-1   Impact of price/volume on market performance.

Once again, the key to the puzzle lies in the mathematics of thrust and momentum. For price to move in one direction on volume that continues rising day after day, there must be some increasingly urgent motivation on the part of buyers or sellers. In the case of an uptrend, more good news, more media exposure, or more excitement on the part of short-term trend-jumping traders is required in order for more buy orders to be created each day. At some point, no more emotional gasoline is being poured onto the fire. The excitement has been played out. My observation is that such upside price moves on highly visible, consistently accelerating volume seldom extend to more than five days.

Phrased in terms of a hold/sell decision question, the operative issue in the short term is, "How can the news or the opinion climate possibly become any more favorable?" When one cannot envision any furtherance of the positive mood, the implied answer fairly shouts: *Sell!* Rising price at some point begins to beget a larger contingent of willing sellers, and it also begins to dissuade the late-arriving would-be buyers. The latter start thinking, "Wow, this thing is up 20 percent in a week—do I really want to chase it at these levels?" That sobering thought plus the lack of new stimulus (news, analysts advising buy) will at some point cool off immediate demand, and therefore volume will stop rising. Short-term traders, keeping their fingers on precisely this pulse measure for the stock, start selling. The price rise is capped and then reversed.

A familiar example of a price rise on a crescendo of rising volume is provided by Pfizer, whose stock was pushed up considerably in the spring of 1998 on news of FDA approval of Viagra, followed by the drug's early commercial success. After four days of extremely heavy and increasing volume, the culmination came when the media reported that more than 40,000 new prescriptions per week were being written. The stock gapped up several points on the opening, traded around $121, had an up day on even higher volume than before—and promptly began a decline that would take it back to $100. How much better could the news become? (At some point, all interested and financially able users would have found doctors to write prescriptions, and bad news would arrive in the sense that fewer new prescriptions were now being written.) Those who might be moved to buy the stock had already heard the story, which was all over the financial media, the tabloids, and the late-night talk shows. Whence would some ever-growing horde of new buyers be manufactured? Thus, a volume crescendo is a strong signal of an imminent price reversal.

VOLUME SPIKES

A volume spike is a more sudden and much larger version of the crescendo. Usually it is triggered by some huge positive news item. The added information is so fundamentally exciting and emotionally persuasive that literally an immediate and huge burst of buying interest forms. Price rockets higher, and trading volume dwarfs any recent past record levels. In the case of several Internet stocks, *daily* trading from November 1998 through early January 1999 actually exceeded total outstanding shares in the companies for one to several days running!

The psychological implications of a spike are even more striking than the fairly clear dynamics of a crescendo. The news is so huge that virtually everyone will be informed and moved to action within a day or so. Can there be follow-on information of even more blockbuster proportions that would cause even *more* investors/traders to buy, thus pushing volume even higher? At extremely high levels, the answer is obviously negative. True, there will be excited newspaper stories covering the news itself and marveling at the spectacular rise in price (while perhaps also mentioning the incredibly large trading volume). You will be highly aware of the reason the stock is up and on everyone's lips. The crucial question is how such excitement, translating into buy orders at market even at now sharply inflated prices, can be sustained and topped tomorrow and the next day. The answer is that it cannot. Therefore immediate sale is warranted.

SUMMARY

This chapter has sought to educate readers on some of the basics of technical analysis—the tracking of price and volume statistics via charting. The purpose has not been to convert you to a chartist or technician, but instead to broaden your awareness and your arsenal of decision-making tools, with particular emphasis on the emotional and psychological content and implications of investor (crowd!) behavior—actions that create the record of price and volume action appearing on the chart. Values govern stock prices in the long term, but emotions and news drive price action in the short term.

Investors, not just traders, can make profitable use of temporary price/volume patterns that typically foretell subsequent price declines. Just as one wants to lighten up on total equities in an extended general market phase, selling on an urgent basis individual stocks that are displaying ominous technical short-term action can provide very attractive exit points. Capital that is not given back to a discouraging subsequent decline is capital preserved to be redeployed for growth later at lower prices—or it can be placed in income-producing assets that will add stability and satisfying, steady cash returns to the owner.

Next time you hear someone reflexively debunk technical analysis as voodoo, you will have a broader knowledge base and can form your own personal judgment more informedly and less emotionally.

7

PSYCHOLOGICAL PREPARATION IS INDISPENSABLE

IF YOU HOPE TO have any chance of avoiding significant damage to your asset base by taking steps to
prepare for market tops, you absolutely must be
psychologically prepared. That means understanding
market psychology and your own investment psychology. And, equally critically, it means being able to sell
your holdings. All of the market history and investment
advice that could fill a library will be useless to you unless
you can take action to reduce your exposure to asset ero-
sion. That action inescapably requires selling some things
you once bought. Good selling is required if you are ever to
take a profit, reduce undue risk, shelter your assets against
declining markets, and reposition assets periodically as your
investment life cycle matures.

This chapter starts by briefly highlighting the importance
of psychological preparation (focusing mainly on preparation
to sell). It then explains 15 external influences and natural

psychological handicaps you must identify in your investment life. Finally, it prescribes specific tactics, approaches,
and actions you must implement to overcome those obstacles
to good selling.

EMOTIONS DRIVE MARKETS' MOVEMENTS

Fundamentals—earnings, cash flows, assets, and dividends—
determine values of securities in the long run. But we live in a
series of todays on the road to that long-run future. A young
investor facing possibly 60 years of market life will live
through some 15,000 market days, adding up at 250 or so per
year. Daily prices in the market—and here note the word *price*
as contrasted with *value*—are determined not by fundamentals
but by the emotions of investors buying and selling on that
particular day. Their emotions are expressed through their
numbers, sizes, and types of buy and sell orders; the balance
of those orders alters price equilibrium. The net urgency of all
orders placed on any one day moves a stock's price to a different level. Price is not value!

On average and over the long term, U.S. stocks tend to
return about 11 to 12 percent per year. Much of that is price
increase, and (especially in recent years) a small fraction—
maybe 2 percent or so—comes from dividend yield. For a
blue-chip-type stock that begins the year at $70, a 9 percent
price gain is equal to about $6.30 per share. If that stock were
to rise by ⅛ point each Friday and close unchanged every other
day of the week, its net rise for the year would be 52 × ⅛, or
$6.50. If you can find a stock which acts that way, buy it! It
will give you great emotional relief from the market's typical
daily gyrations. (People buy CDs because of such comfort, but
then pay a terrible price for that feeling of assurance in the
form of low or negative real after-tax returns.) As you well
know, stocks simply do not ratchet up gradually with no setbacks. All the daily and weekly price fluctuations that make
the stock market newsworthy are simply flashy, short-term
changes much more volatile than either the underlying

improvement in value or the average expected net price rise. Price fluctuations far exceeding net change in value are driven by investors' emotions, whether those investors be faceless individuals or famous professionals managing billions of dollars of other people's money. Emotions get out of whack, alternately on the upside and the downside.

Bull markets that extend well beyond any rational measure of realistic value reflect collective overoptimism, fantasy, inertia, and greed. Protecting equity capital from the inevitable negative swing to collective overpessimism requires first identifying signs of a too-bubbly market and then taking action in response. If you are unable to sell to take advantage of temporary excess enthusiasm by others, you should put all your equity money into index funds and vow never to look at the market's daily movements until you need to sell, either eventually to reduce the risk profile of your asset mix or to live on the proceeds. Dedicated long-term holders are fated to achieve average-at-best returns—but only if they are lucky and have enough self-control not to panic and sell in a low market. Because they will never take advantage of transient, unrealistically high phases, their best hope is to achieve the market's long-term average returns in the long run. Such investors have no need for reading investment books.

The only way you can capture returns in excess of average (which at the same time shields your capital against future interim returns below average!) is to be willing to sell. If you are unwilling to sell, you will be unable to do the following:

- Capture big gains from manias before they disappear (Chapter 3)
- Take advantage of developing tops you identify in individual stocks, industry groups, or the overall market (Chapter 5)
- Be able to reposition your assets, either moderately or significantly, in anticipation of market cycles (Chapters 8 and 9)

- Shift among mutual funds at proper times in life (Chapters 10 and 11)

- Implement tax-smart tactics now or in retirement (Chapter 12)

Think of it this way: if you cannot bring yourself to the point of being psychologically able to sell, you are a prisoner in a jail of your own construction. If you cannot sell, you are doomed to owning your present portfolio until you die. You'd better hope those companies' health is better than yours, for longer!

Having identified the crucial need to master investment psychology in order to be able to sell (and sell well), let's move on to understanding market emotions and to taking actions that will help you avoid unnecessary losses and achieve better-than-average long-term results.

INVESTMENT PSYCHOLOGY 101

Just as human beings' behavior reflects both their innate drives (nature) and their experiences (nurture), so investors face sets of both internal and external biases and stimuli that influence their investing behaviors. Successful investing is not an especially natural process for humans, so we must clearly identify and then constantly work to overcome factors that prompt counterproductive financial behavior. In the next few pages, we will identify and explore 15 influences or factors that shape our investment choices and actions. A few of these are external stimuli, but most are internal self-handicapping tendencies and biases. Following the cataloging and explanation, we will work on practical actions and steps you can take to overcome those obstacles.

IDENTIFYING AND UNDERSTANDING EXTERNAL STIMULI

Brokers.   Except for those rare birds who are true contrarians, brokers are likely to create more problems than assistance for investors seeking to sell stocks to reduce risk in high markets.

First, structurally, traditional full-commission brokers are in a position of conflict. Their investment banking or corporate finance divisions have relationships with companies that periodically need additional financing. Keeping those relationships constructive requires that brokerage research departments never express negative opinions. Few brokerage firms permit their analysts to say "sell" in print! So do not expect to get help from brokerage firms in deciding either when the market is high or which stocks to sell off.* The very common "hold" advice actually is "sell" in disguise, but advice to hold is mistakenly perceived as too clear and positive to interpret in exactly the opposite way.

Second, brokers are systematically encouraged by their firms to sell you the "product of the month" (or week). Whenever you raise cash (perhaps in your move to lighten equity exposure in a high market), brokers will see your capital as available to invest in their latest offering. You will need firm resolve to resist such suggestions and carry out your contrarian intentions.

Third, when a broker is not selling the designated company-backed new issue, he or she is likely to be watching the hottest stocks or groups in the market. Sharing their enthusiasm over what is hot is a way of hooking you into taking action in exactly those stocks and groups you should be exiting. While what is hot is already pricey, it is also familiar and therefore an easy sale. Gold and gold stocks were the rage in 1980. Internet stocks at hundreds of times revenue(!) were irresistible in the spring of 1999. Successful salesmanship involves selling the client what is easy to sell. Very hot stocks are always easy for a broker to sell, just when they are predictably living on borrowed time. The way to a commission in a hot market is to mirror and then feed off a client's greed and excitement. This is not a road you want to follow while trying to cut back exposure to risk.

---

*An SEC study released in April 1999 documented that 64 percent of research reports said "buy," while under 2 percent said "sell."

Full-service brokerage commission rates act as barriers to taking action. While your enthusiasm over an exciting new idea seldom is blocked by commission aversion, for a variety of reasons a decision to sell out usually is readily subject to veto because of the cost of exit. We immediately see the selling commission as part of our assets given away, and we can easily calculate the amount in per-share terms. This makes it hard to agree to pull the selling trigger. If you continue to do business with full-commission brokerage firms, you must develop the mind-set that commissions will never become an issue for you when your proper course is to sell off stocks to lighten up. This will prove very difficult to implement.

The traditional media. We always know (with remarkably perfect hindsight!) why a stock or group or the overall market is up (or down). The print and electronic media report the latest vivid happenings, but never the mundane or boring stuff. They focus on extremes (how fast the Dow Jones Industrials have gained their latest 1000 points, or how many points a hot technology stock jumped yesterday, or how much the market is up so far this year or in the last few weeks' run). They report with excitement the glowing earnings report and the newest gee-whiz technology that is pushing a stock into a price/earnings stratosphere. The daily and weekly media deal in newsbites, virtually never providing useful context. History and context are not exciting or juicy enough to deserve coverage, and the media are shy of providing advice anyway. In a high market, media behavior acts to reinforce existing biases toward holding big gainers, tempting investors to jump onto bandwagons late, when prices are high. The media, in sum, reinforce through repetition what is obvious. In so doing, they keep stockholders increasingly comfortable as prices go higher and tempt us to plunge (out of greed and/or frustration) at just the wrong time. (Conversely, in a declining phase, the media reinforce or heighten our late-developing fears and this prompts our ill-timed selling.)

The Internet.   Although a wonderful new information tool for investors and traders, the Internet can also subtly but strongly encourage crowd following and speculation. Those are exactly the kinds of behavior a disciplined investor must seek to avoid in a high market. Vast, readily available information makes its acquirer feel highly informed. Like the conventional media, the Internet reinforces the latest great news and the current upward price trend, but it does so with added immediacy and thrill. Chat rooms, even if deliberate touters could be banished, would still be fertile ground for excitement and rumor, which feed greed and thereby thwart our good intentions about reducing risk exposure. Sharers of investment ideas on the Net tend overwhelmingly to support and explain the existing trend, thus raising listeners' willingness to buy or hold rather than to sell out in a high market. Seeing heady moment-to-moment price movement encourages investors to become traders in what appears to be an easy game. The immediacy of a six-day rally makes it seem obvious that this stock has big support and will keep running. Tick-by-tick drama urges the greedy juices toward joining the crowd in an attractive game. Being able to take action by pressing a few keys, with no human buffer available, encourages speculating. The most positive facet of Internet trading is its extremely low on-line commissions, which can help you overcome a major force inhibiting selling. But on balance, the Internet has added to the external psychological sources of stimulus that condition loss-inducing investor behavior.

Colleagues and friends.   In our work settings and in our social environments, we associate with people whom we've come to trust. Unfortunately, most nonprofessional investors underperform the markets—or actually lose net money. Thus, by listening to others we expose ourselves to influences not likely on average to be helpful. Friends and col- leagues often brag of their (usually still paper) winnings in high markets, but rarely admit to jumping in late and already being down 12 points on a hot stock. Thus, in a high-market period our associates act like the media, the hot-idea brokers, and the Internet in reinforcing "reasons" to stay fully in- vested and/or to take a flyer on a shooting star. Colleagues and friends provide this damaging function quite innocently, but their influence is strong. Partly because we trust our friends and colleagues workers, we believe a friend's bro- ker's idea because it is already working, although we might have questioned our own broker's motivation if he or she had provided the same suggestion.

Colleagues and friends also can be very damaging influ- ences if we talk about our contrarian, risk-reducing moves late in a bull cycle. "How can you stand to miss the action?" or "Why did you already sell that star performer on the way up (and too soon)?" they ask. In so doing, they innocently but forcefully argue to undo the calculated risk-reducing steps we have taken before the final top has become obvious. (These friends and co-workers will do likewise, in reverse, at and near bottoms by expressing their great fears and repeat- ing well-known negative reasons—and they might well scare us out of having more courage than they do and thereby keep us from buying bargains. But that's a story for another time, since our focus here is on preparing for and dealing with *toppy* markets.)

As much as the preceding four groups and forces exert external stimulus on us that hurts our chances for taking proper market action, we face an even more daunting array of often-invisible internal drives and emotions that undercut our investment success. These are our next topics for discussion.

INTERNAL PSYCHOLOGICAL HINDRANCES
Greed.   Described more gently or politely as our apparently compulsive and relentless desire to acquire, greed is a major

enemy for investors and traders alike. Greed is stoked by a rising market and, of course, is predictably most virulent when markets are hottest. All around us stories abound of easy money being made fast: multiple-point daily gains, triple-digit daily advances by the Dow Jones Industrials, hundreds of new highs listed in the newspaper, an engaging interview with this month's (or week's) hottest fund manager. Fear is a stronger emotion than greed, as shown in a variety of life situations and by numerous academic experiments. Before, at, and for some while after a market bottom, fear will paralyze our urge to buy an apparent bargain, thus overwhelming greed. Later, at market tops, we will buy at 40 what we feared at 15; the good news is so plentiful and the media and brokerage cheering sections so loud that just when caution is most in order, we are most prone to ignore any nagging fears (about historically high P/E ratios or low yields) and stay fully invested, because making money quickly is so much fun. (See Figure 7-1.) Extremes in or culminations of stocks' price moves are defined by the runaway victory of greed over fear (tops) or the reverse (bottoms). These can be seen in sharp price movements and in extremely heavy trading volume. Such do not characterize middle, more orderly stages of market moves because at those times the two competing emotional forces are in much more nearly even opposition.

Ego.   A degree of ego is a good thing, but too much is dangerous. Our egos are stroked when we are correct, when we win, when we make money. When we make a mistake, all too

When Stocks Are . . .	We Perceive Risk As Being . . .	But Actually Risk Is Then . . .
High	Low	High
Low	High	Low

FIGURE 7-1   Recurring misperceptions of risk.

often we refuse to acknowledge it to ourselves or to out-
siders. (This can be a powerful argument not only for *not*
sharing one's investment details with friends, but also for
using an impersonal discount broker rather than a familiar
human with whom there must be stress- or pain-generating
interaction.) High markets make our egos feel great. When a
market is rolling over, or when a formerly skyrocketing stock
or group heads south, we have a very difficult time admitting
we've made wrong choices. Repeated wins in a strong (late-
stage) bull phase raise a healthy sense of ego to an unrealistic state of pride and feelings of invincibility. A good stock
we have held for a major gain is a source of ego stroking, and
that subtle relationship between our stock and our ego makes
any decision to sell all the more difficult. Ego creates an
affinity bond that thwarts our ability to separate. We adopt
our winning stock as a family member or beloved pet.

Perfectionism.   This tendency is related to ego, but has also
been externally conditioned (and then internalized) by our
professional and business and academic experiences. Parents
want us to get all As; employers give bonuses for zero-defects
performance; we bask in adulation for crowning professional
and intellectual victories. We are thrilled and inspired by athletes who get a perfect score. We live for a hole in one. All
these things encourage us to want to be excellent, which is not
a bad thing. Striving to be perfect pushes us past the usual
boundaries of human capacity. The good feedback we get
from great success makes us hungry (dare we say *greedy?*) for
more. More than great is perfect, but perfection is unrealistic.

We readily tolerate buying a stock at less than a perfect
price because our ownership period is open-ended, which
offers hope of repairing any early damage and eventually
coming out with a prized win, a gain, a proof of our brilliance. Selling represents a finalizing of the result: you
gained or lost exactly so much, precisely documented by the
computer and clearly visible to broker, spouse, and accoun-

tant—and, most vividly, to you! We'd like to sell at the highest price, although that level is reached in reality only for a moment or two on one day out of 250 trading sessions per year. The odds of a perfectly priced sale are extremely high against us, and yet our ego and the external conditioning about excellence that we've internalized push us to demand perfection of ourselves. It's a very powerful influence working against selling in an advancing market. And if our stock is already below its recent better levels, we have clear proof we've failed to be perfect, and therefore selling after the high is ever harder to do! We need to identify and battle perfectionist tendencies and be realistic about our human imperfection. That is easy to say in the abstract, but when money and ego are on the line, perfectionism is difficult to overcome. Perfectionist behavior is a major cause of failure to reduce risk exposure in high but ever-tempting markets.

Closure avoidance.   This is seldom discussed, but very real. Part of our aversion to coming to closure is strongly tied to the aforementioned perfectionist tendencies. We run late in submitting that report at work because we imagine more time might bring us one more key insight or fact to include. We know that once the project is finished and made available to others we cannot any longer improve or perfect it. Openendedness keeps hope alive. But closures in our lives have often been sad times, and therefore we tend to resist such situations. Leaving our alma mater and its friendly associations and relatively less demanding lifestyle was a bittersweet time. Moving across the country for a new job meant leaving our circle of comforting friends, our carefully customized home's charming familiarity, those dependable merchants and maintenance people, and a known safe neighborhood. Saying good-bye at a funeral, needless to say, is a closure consistently associated with pain. Cleaning out the attic at Great-Grandma's and selling the family farm bring tears and heartache, no matter how we try to focus on remembering and savoring the good times. Finally, when we sell stocks, we are closing down our freedom to make any further decision about holding versus selling. We are stepping up and hitting a bold return shot that will render our move clearly a winner or a loser. By refusing to sell, by refusing to make closure, we leave possibilities invitingly open. This is a subtle but very real tug against selling that we must surface and battle.

Comfort-zone retention. Not unrelated to our aversion to closure, and serving our egos, our greed, and our hopes for being perfect, we savor our comfort zones once we find them. The better a stock or fund has treated us, and the longer the time it's done so, the more strongly we quietly adopt it as a beloved family member, mascot, or pet. Think of the great growth stocks (McDonald's, Microsoft, or Philip Morris, perhaps—although the nasty realist inside me prompts my adding, from another era, University Computing, Polaroid, Memorex, and Winnebago). When we own the great winners (or the historically strong funds), we revolt at the idea of giving them up; it's an insult to our sense of investment wholeness, an attack on (buy-and-hold) religion and Mother's apple pie. Where else will we go? How will we feel if we sell our winner and it moves even higher? No, we'll take our chances with a proven friend! Of course, as a market's rise becomes greater in time and/or percentage terms, the comfort-zone pull against selling out or moving into uncharted territory becomes ever more powerful. Good news aplenty continues to support our resolve to hold (just as, near bear-market bottoms, widespread doses of fearful events and risks deter us from buying stocks at prices that later will prove to be absolute steals). We must recognize this comfort-zone pull and keep trying to battle it hardest when it becomes most strong!

Pain avoidance. Numerous controlled experiments have demonstrated that we value avoiding pain even more strongly than we seek and desire pleasure or gain or reward. Selling stocks, particularly in a market that is palpably fun to continue playing in, threatens to bring us pain in several ways. First, we suspect we'll soon see our sold stock move higher, meaning a loss of further gains (which of course will frustrate our greed for more, more!). Second, that run-up after we sell will remind us of our imperfection, dealing a blow to our ego. And of course, we will incur those despised taxes and commissions if we sell out. Further, if we're foolish enough to tell our friends that we've sold and then prices do move higher, they will taunt us with their further gains and our lack of faith. That will really hurt! The pain of selling too soon (which is clearly obvious and immediate when it happens) is more vivid than the theoretical pain of loss we might have if we hold on and it turns out we really should have sold. A pain in hand today hurts many times more than a possible hurt in the undefined future. We just will not be able to stand it if we sell our Microsoft and see it 10 points higher in a couple of weeks. Missing the game will be no fun at all!

Stress avoidance.   Our Sunday magazine articles, our physicians, and a lot of advertising all urge us to reduce stress as much as possible. Deliberately *not* selling serves to reduce stress in visible ways, at least for today. We will not need to make a decision or pay a commission or pony up some estimated taxes on our gain. We will not need to worry about seeing that stock keep riding higher without us on board. We will not need to doubt ourselves, nor will we hear our friends second-guess us. We will not need to deal with feelings of imperfection, of wishing we'd never given up our comfortable relationship with that ego-stroking winner. And, subtly but not at all a small issue, we will not need to face the stress of deciding how to reinvest the dollars freed up via that sale.

Nostalgia.   Ah, for the good ol' days! Or was that the good old daze? Sometimes we look through rose-colored glasses at good times past. This stock has treated us so well for so long. At least it treated us well for a good while. Can it really now be a bad thing to continue holding (close to our bosom and cuddling fondly)? Reality is that times and companies and technologies and competitive positions and currency values change—much as we'd wish they would just hold still and make our investment lives simpler. We hark back to, and hope to regain, happier times. Those times are definable (the stock made X percent over N years), whereas a future without that stock is unknowable. That stock (or fund) is pretty familiar to us, while literally 10,000 others out there represent the less known. A good stock is like an old and trusted friend. Sure, it had its ups and downs and gave us a few scary moments on the way up, but as they say, the devil you know versus one you don't! All of this makes it very difficult to sell after a long and strong uptrending market. And the strength of our positive feelings toward our old reliables becomes even more compelling just as the danger inherent in not parting with them (as they fall from even more overpriced levels) grows greater. Watch out for nostalgic feelings.

Mourning.   We mourn what is lost, and we mourn what might have been. In terms of investment decisions in a mature bull market, mourning can take several forms, and it is intimately related to some of the psychological issues already described. First, it's quite often true that if we have losses after a considerable bull-market run, those losses reflect companies with problems. We hesitate to sell them, because doing so certifies our fallibility (we made a mistake) and brings closure to that episode (there now can definitely be no redemption, no correction, no recovery). We mourn the blow to our ego that recognizing, admitting, and accepting a mistake brings. And where there's a gain rather than a loss, we mourn in advance for what we view as the likelihood of further gains forgone (just "knowing" that when we sell, that stock will turn on and punish us with a personally insulting rise). So we are mourning our inability to be perfect, even though we know at an intellectual level that such is unrealistic and impossible. And if perchance we've already seen our stock or a major industry group or the market as a whole fall more than just a bit from recent high levels, we are mourning over the dollars in paper profit given up and over our real or imagined lack of expertise in selling out at the top. "I just knew when it hit 120 I should have sold!" Did you really, or were you looking eagerly to 140 and a possible stock split? Sometimes we imagine ourselves having come closer to pulling the selling trigger at a propitious moment than was actually the real truth at the time. We are mourning our lack of perfect foresight, which we wish we had. Whatever the nature or specifics of our mourning, taking action to sell out seems to imply making our pain more acute and vivid, while taking inaction gives us at least some slim hope for a cure, some chance that it might all work out well in the end.

Rationalization: commissions.   The nine items just discussed were all emotions and attitudes and mind-sets. The next two are behaviors. Both are subtly and subconsciously designed to allow us to not make a decision, to not come to closure, to not admit a mistake, to not close off the chances that our greed and ego might be better fed if our stock rises further. Both of these rationalizations, or cover stories for not taking action to sell, also allow us to shift or at least share the blame.

Commissions are, of course, necessary unless you invest in an Exchange membership and then can trade free. Commissions were part of the rules of the game that you well understood when you decided to become an investor. But now, when it is time to sell out to reduce risk exposure, or at least to seriously consider such action and maybe to at least place a stop-loss order, resentment at paying the broker can be used as a reason for taking no action in your own interest. "He helped me get into this loser, and now I'm expected to pay *again* to escape?" Or, when the stock is up, "Look what a percentage of my gain her round-trip commission robs me of!" Or, when the successful idea was entirely yours, "Why should I be forced to share part of my winnings with that useless bystander?" Maybe the commodities markets have it figured out better: there, one pays a round-trip commission upon opening a position: pulling the trigger to close it out costs nothing "extra" at that moment. No matter what form the commission-avoidance rationalization takes or where it comes from, the end result is *not* making a decision. There certainly are ways to overcome this problem, as will be covered shortly.

Rationalization: taxes.   Like commissions, taxes were part of the rules before you entered the investment arena. They are not a new wrinkle, not a whole new dimension, not new rules suddenly introduced at halftime. So it is unrealistic (and actually a disservice to your own interests) to raise aversion to taxes as a "reason" you (supposedly) cannot or will not sell. Once again, as with many of the underlying emotions and triggers, the tax-aversion impulse is strongest and therefore most difficult to overcome when stocks are highest (exactly when your gains and thus tax liabilities are greatest). Income tax avoidance makes sense mainly for a person with a fatal illness. It might make sense for someone with a huge long-term gain on paper. Otherwise, there is no rational reason for using the widely publicized tax excuse. Again, the bottom line is that tax avoidance allows you a socially and internally forgivable reason for doing nothing. Like the commission ploy, tax-aversion rationalizing also allows you to share the blame for inaction with an evil "other." "If only the Feds and the state did not want to suck my pockets clean with taxes, I'd be willing to sell this stock while it's up. My unwillingness to sell now is mainly their fault." If only, if only!

CONTROLLING AND OVERCOMING THESE
DETRIMENTAL INFLUENCES

The preceding pages have defined, illuminated, and illustrated the externally occurring and self-created sources of difficulty with selling we have as investors—forces that impede our rational and more profitable behavior in advanced bull markets and with big-winner individual stocks. Now we will move to solutions for these problems. The first step in overcoming such self-defeating influences is to identify them. When a market is advanced, in terms you have identified clearly from what you learned in Chapters 3 through 5, it is time to review carefully your list of stocks and funds to identify what must be sold. You will almost certainly have subconscious or vague "reasons" or feelings why just about every stock is not a candidate for sale.

It would be a good exercise to pretend you absolutely must immediately raise X dollars or Y percent of your net worth in cash (not that you will actually do it in one day). Faced with that arbitrarily imposed requirement, you will need to examine more critically your motivations and hesitations regarding each stock. You might well use the 15 issues discussed earlier as a checklist of behavioral warning signs (see Figure 7-2). That will help you see concretely where your resistance to selling is coming from, both on individual stocks and as a common or recurring pattern. It will be a useful exercise to sit down and put aside all distractions and analyze every holding at one time. That way you will not lose discipline with a fuzzy promise to look at the rest "sometime soon." In what follows, we will not rehash the nature of the problems. Rather, we will bluntly and with hard-hitting sharpness prescribe attitudes to adopt and remedial or overcoming actions to take.

THE EXTERNAL STIMULI

Brokers

Attitudes and approaches.   Remember that your broker is most useful only when he or she acts as a buffer against your

	Stock A	Stock B
1. Brokers		
2. Traditional-media noise		
3. Internet excitement		
4. Friends' influences		
5. Greed		
6. Ego		
7. Perfectionism		
8. Closure avoidance		
9. Comfort-zone retention		
10. Pain avoidance		
11. Stress avoidance		
12. Nostalgia		
13. Mourning		
14. Commissions as rationalization		
15. Taxes as rationalization		

FIGURE 7-2   **Personal-warning checklist of barriers to selling.**

crowd-following impulses. Note also that his or her ticket to a paycheck is to get you to take action; feeding your emotions will make it easy to get you to trade. That means your broker may try tapping your greed and excitement in a hot market, which you need to resist allowing.

Actions.   Reject all hot ideas; your job is to reduce risk rather than add to it. Never take action without literally sleeping on an idea. Never buy any initial public offering (IPO) that a broker offers to you (ones they can get easily will not go up). Reject ideas on replacement stocks to buy with proceeds of sales you've just made: your proper course is to shift into different asset classes! Get a flat-rate deep-discount broker so you can avoid the commission-driven broker's unhelpful interactions and intrusions into your strategic execution, and so you will moot commission rationalization.

The Traditional Media

Attitudes and approaches.   Remember at all times that the media repeat dramatic and familiar stories, and that this tends to put you into a false comfort zone. Determine to watch the media not for the detailed minutia of stories but instead to identify the psychological content and the influence their stories carry or extend. Recognize that the media try to explain rather than question obvious facts such as runaway market trends. Ignore and play contrary to supposed experts who say, "It's different this time: all the old yardsticks are outmoded." (Basing decisions on this wayward but seductive adage will lead you astray.)

Actions.   Never follow the direction of a media story. If you take any action, insist that it be to sell, rather than buy, into strength on a bullish story. Watch for extremes in reporting and on magazine covers (the bull roaring up an incline!) and for supposed authorities being quoted as predicting continuation of the long-established trend. When you see these forever-repeated patterns, slice off some stocks and cut your exposure promptly. When you're told, "It's different this time, stocks are really not high at all," chuckle quietly and do some selling without delay.

The Internet

Attitudes and approaches.   View the Internet in two sharply distinct ways. First, use it positively to do research on ideas you have that had their origins elsewhere. Second, negatively view the Internet as a megaphone for the mob's wildness, as a sensitive barometer of the intensity of collective market emotions. When the prevailing opinion is shrill and uniform, when everyone has unanimously bullish ideas and predictions, sell aggressively! View all urgent recommendations of stocks to buy as probable touts.

Actions. Never follow crowd opinion, which forms most strongly only late in a trend. When the Internet is loaded with optimists and get-rich-quick schemes, do some selling. Use charts available free on the Internet to examine individual stocks for volume spikes accompanying sharp price advances, and for volume parabolas or crescendos pushing rising prices. These are great times to sell! Also, use free Internet charts of sector mutual funds to identify unsustainable upside price momentum or gradual rounding tops: both are signs of time to sell. Fidelity and INVESCO both have numerous industry and sector funds; tape a list of their five-letter ticker symbols to your computer screen's frame.

Colleagues and Friends

Attitudes and approaches. While you may like these folks, remember that they're not experts, and that they tell you only the good and not the bad things they do in the market. In microcosm, they represent the crowd you need to avoid joining; keep this in mind when there's a lot of market buzz around the watercooler.

Actions. Don't take advice from these folks. Don't take the advice of their brokers or other advisors. Use these folks as contrary indicators: when they are celebrating and telling you how fast they're getting rich, silently nail down some of your profits fast so you *stay* rich. If you have a particularly manic-depressive type of friend, secretly use his or her most strident opinions as red-flag contrary signals! Don't tell your colleagues and friends about your investments, so you will not later need to withstand verbal heat from them when they think you have sold too early in a frothy market.

THE INTERNAL PSYCHOLOGICAL HINDRANCES

Greed

Attitudes and approaches.   Realize that greed is a nearly universal human attitude, and one that often serves us badly. Understand that greed will be most intense when the pot is boiling, which is exactly when you most urgently need to take chips off the table to reduce your risk of loss. Know that *that* will be hard to do. Understand that the more psychological discomfort a market action produces, the more likely it is to prove financially sound. Recognize above-average greed in yourself and other market participants close to you, and take it as a strong warning signal to stimulate selling actions.

Actions.   After stocks have risen for more than two years, ignore good news. Never raise your price targets. Observe sharp rises or runs of many consecutive days, and sell when these occur, just when you're most proud and pleased! Sell immediately whenever you say to yourself, "I'm going to sell in one more day" or "after I get just one more point." That is raw greed talking, and it never utters a peep in a low or depressed market.

Ego

Attitudes and approaches.   Become realistic: understand that we all must have some ego/confidence or we'd never have ventured beyond bank CDs and money market funds to try to win in this exciting game. But know that your ego, as it expands, will both signal a high market and get in the way of proper action.

Actions.   As soon as you stroke your ego by counting the chips or the profits, sell some stocks! As soon as you brag to your spouse or to folks at the office or the club about your market victories, use that as a sure sign of a high market and do some selling. If you start thinking of quitting your day job to manage your money full time, do some serious bailing out. Your ego brags near tops, not bottoms. Listen to it, and run upon its warning!

Perfectionism

Attitudes and approaches.   Understand our natural desire to be excellent and, at the extreme, never to make a mistake. And then remember the human condition: we are inherently fallible. Come to accept that reality, and your market operations will become remarkably easier and less stressful. Give up on trying to be being perfect; waiting to get the final information or execute the perfect exit will doom you to staying in the market forever, well down from and after the forming top. Adopt the attitude that pretty good is good but perfect is a destructively impossible standard.

Actions.   Set selling targets above the market before you buy a stock. This will prevent you from having open-ended expectations of unending glory. Enter orders a fraction below those round-dollar levels as soon as you have bought. Watch for rationalization, holding onto favorites because they make you feel so good, and reaching for "just one more point." Sell some stocks when you see these behaviors in yourself or others.

Closure Avoidance

Attitudes and approaches.   Remember the reasons that coming to closure often makes us feel bad. And then force yourself to come to decisions. Be demanding on yourself rather than indulgently forgiving of indecision. Read and take advice from a good book on overcoming procrastination.

Actions.   Again, set a sell order in place as soon as you receive your purchase confirmation. This will create a habitual, mechanical device that will help you avoid the stress of making a decision later. Selling a stock up will be hard if you try to do it *ad hoc,* but entering a selling-limit order will make it easy and automatic. Set trailing stop orders below the price, at levels that would represent technical-formation breakdowns. Again, forcing yourself to put these devices in place will prevent you from adopting indecision and inaction as your operating mode.

Comfort-Zone Retention

Attitudes and approaches.   Recognize that you will subconsciously favor keeping those stocks that have treated you best, but that this tendency is based on financially illogical reasoning and occurs most strongly at just the wrong times—when those stocks and the market are dangerously extended. Ask yourself if holding will keep you comfortable. If it will, then sell. Ask yourself if selling will make you uncomfortable (fearful and regretful about missing more of the fun). Do what will make you *uncomfortable.*

Actions.   Sell stocks regularly, whenever they have recently given you an unreasonably large or fast profit. Learn to get out of your comfort zone richer but less comfortable in the process. Selling even your winners regularly will keep you paying taxes as you go and later (when the market is far extended) will keep you from letting tax phobia become your excuse for staying in a comfort zone by surrounding yourself with stroking winners.

Pain Avoidance

Attitudes and approaches.   Tie this one to perfectionism and ego. Accept the idea that you will have a batting average far from 1000. Get used to the idea that you *will* take losses, and remember that quite often the first loss will prove to be by far the best one to accept. Remember: every time you make a mistake (at least in your taxable account), the taxing authorities will mitigate part of it if you will just admit the problem and move on.

Actions. Place stop orders so that when one of your stocks drops, you will not need to deal with the emotional hurt of making a decision about holding versus selling. Let the market take you out before you reach a painful threshold at a much lower, scary price level. Place target sell orders above the market so you will be sold out on a rally and not need to endure the later pain of thinking, "If only I'd sold up at X."

Stress Avoidance

Attitudes and approaches. Accept the fact that dealing in the investment markets is by nature a stress-inducing activity. Accept the need to deal with this stress, because the alternative is being poorer for having lived in the stress-free, low-return environment of CDs and money market funds. Recognize that if you do not deal with small stresses frequently, you may end up with terrible investment failures that will cause major stress in a very late, panicky exit and will cause major stress with your spouse and from your reduced standard of retirement living. Trade repeated encounters with small decisions against huge stroke-inducing worries put off but eventually unavoidably faced. Again, seeking comfort (or avoiding pain) by evading a decision will be the wrong thing.

Actions. As prescribed, use above-market limits and below-market protective stops as artificial devices that will assure decisions in advance—before the stress of the moment makes you want to run away and avoid any decision. Practice occasionally trading for a short-term gain in a stock where you have confidence. Each trading buy will be made with some assurance that the main trend is up and will rescue you. Each sell will be made with the knowledge that this will not be "good-bye forever," and each pulling of the selling trigger will reduce the stress level of taking such an actions in future situations.

Nostalgia

Attitudes and approaches.   Recognize that change is the rule rather than the exception, regardless of our preference that it be otherwise. Realize that a business does not succeed today or tomorrow on its past glory, but only on its newest ideas and technology and competitive thrusts. Therefore, expect that some once-great companies and stocks will falter and become shadows of their former selves. Resolve not to fall in love and forgive all the way down the slippery slope. Recognize and accept that your portfolio must change as the world does and as your life-stage needs dictate.

Actions.   Ask yourself a demanding question: Would you buy this stock today at its present price? If you would not, you are living on past glory with an investment partner that is becoming weaker or that is overpriced based on today's realities. What you would not buy today, you should not hold. Holding, you see, is merely passive recommitment (or, if you will, passive buying again) of the portfolio you were holding when the day began. What you would not buy, you ought to sell!

Mourning

Attitudes and approaches.   Adopt a view of investments that parallels life: nothing is forever. You must do the best you can and then move on. Not all investments will work, nor will even the good ones be perfect forever. You will rarely sell at the exact top, any more than you bought at the exact bottom. So allow yourself not to worry about perfect executions not accomplished: learn to celebrate the above-average though not perfectly optimal returns that you actually do nail down. Don't mourn in advance and overstay the top, and don't mourn paper profits given back.

Actions.   Set your sell targets and protective stop orders, and live out life free from constant what-if's. When you sell, albeit imperfectly, in a clearly extended and thus risky market, focus on all the assets you did protect and the grief you will avoid rather than on the smaller amounts you did not perfectly capture. Move confidently into safer asset classes rather than looking back and wishing you'd sold perfectly.

Rationalization: Commissions

Attitudes and approaches.   Forget about commissions, because they are a part of the process that cannot be avoided. Never allow commission considerations to deflect you from action. If you catch yourself using commissions as a rationalization for taking no action, forbid that behavior, knowing that you will eventually need to pay a commission—at either a higher or lower price.

Actions.   If you find yourself thinking about the amount of the commission, you are paying too much commission. The only way to stop that is to move to a flat-rate, deep-discount broker. You *must* get commissions out of the equation when considering hold versus sell. When there is no apparent urgency to sell immediately, and the stock or market is trending sideways within normal fluctuation limits, enter your would-be market orders slightly above the last trade. When the market comes to your price, you will have offset your commission cost with good execution. On the margin, this improves your net returns. And it makes taking each action feel satisfying rather than painfully costly.

Rationalization: Taxes

Attitudes and approaches.   Recall that taxes are not a surprising or new factor in the investment equation (assuming you bought this stock since 1913, when the Internal Revenue Code was first enacted). Forbid yourself from using taxes as an excuse to escape taking sale action. Focus on the fact that your goal was to make a profit so you can live better. View any given profit goal such as "10 points" as actually meaning "10 points before required taxes." Strive to pay a lot of taxes, because it means you have captured a lot of profits before they melted away from "paper" to "former paper" in nature. Remember: the two most effective ways to never pay taxes are to have lots of losses—or to die!

Actions.   Ignore taxes, except when you are a very few days shy of moving from the short-term to the long-term holding period (and thus in the narrow time window that implies limited risk of giving back major price gains). View the favorable long-term-gains tax rate as *a bonus rather than an entitlement.* If you catch yourself using tax aversion as a rationalization for not selling, forbid yourself that silly luxury and force yourself to identify another reason not to sell. Then, be sure that reason is not among those described in this chapter!

SUMMARY

This chapter has exposed the long list of obstacles we all face when needing to reposition assets and reduce risks. You absolutely must overcome these self-defeating hang-ups and recurring behavior patterns. If you cannot sell, you will die with your present portfolio. If you cannot sell well, you will repeatedly sell poorly. The choice is yours. The payoffs from your choice and your efforts at behavior modification will be a more satisfying stock market experience now and greater financial freedom in the future.

8

IDENTIFYING AND RANKING YOUR VULNERABILITIES

ONGRATULATIONS . . . YOU'RE ALREADY MORE than halfway there! You've learned of the critical importance of preparing for and cutting exposure to bear markets. You've read the history of bull markets, so you understand their approximate heights and especially lengths. You've seen the usually rounding shape of a general market top and marveled at the often spiky tops made by individual stocks and industry groups. You've wrestled with the tough psychological issues you must overcome to be able to sell, because repositioning assets is impossible otherwise.

Now, being emotionally able to carry out some selling and having a greatly improved sense of when that is the wise course, you are probably asking this: "Where are my weakest points—where I can get hurt the worst?" And then, "How do I actually go about reducing my risk exposure, either moderately or in a major way?" This chapter and the next will address those issues.

REMINDER: IT'S AN ART RATHER THAN A SCIENCE

Because no two bull markets are quite the same, it should be no surprise that no two bear phases will prove totally alike. They will differ regarding length (time), depth (percent lost), and character (which kinds of stocks and funds fare worse than which others). It would be impossible to rank every asset class and every industry on a precise scale from most vulnerable to least at risk and expect that list to play out in perfect order in the next down market, or in any specific one after that. But in the next few pages we will lay out general patterns that will prevail in most cases.

Major exceptions to these typical risk rankings will usually be driven by the triggering event or cause that ended the bull market, and by how different types of stocks performed during the latest upward phase. For example, the 1990 decline was led by financial issues, which suffered fierce losses in the wake of the bank and S&L crises. The 1998 smash of roughly 2000 Dow points in just 11 weeks crunched stocks of companies with significant overseas business and/or large financing requirements; fears of a worldwide recession and credit meltdown were the trigger. Back in 1973–1974, industries and companies most adversely affected by spiraling energy and raw materials costs, and those sensitive to inflation and high interest rates, were the worst victims. Details differ every time, but the pattern of worst losers is predictably constant.

A SYSTEMATIC APPROACH FOR IDENTIFYING
YOUR ACHILLES' HEELS

We'll look at riskiness or vulnerability in several separate ways. First, taking a top-down approach, we will briefly identify asset classes most likely to suffer in a down market or ("in case" one actually occurs) in an economic contraction. Then we will turn to a listing of sectors and industries and cluster them from most to relatively least risky. Next, we will study the personality characteristics of various stocks in yet another angle on identifying unusual risk potentials. And finally, because so many investors hold so much of their equity (and bond) portfolios in the form of mutual funds rather than only in individual securities, we will place major types of funds on a continuum from generally most risky to generally less so.

This approach will enable you to then categorize your securities and funds on each dimension studied, and thereby to develop a sense of how highly exposed you are overall. It will also help you to focus on which specific holdings seem to have the greatest (and least) chances of biting you in a down market.

RISKS OF ASSET CLASSES

Here we are expanding a bit the usual shortest-possible list of major asset types (stocks, bonds, cash, and hard assets) to bring out more subtleties and dimensions in some of those four groupings. Table 8-1 highlights the special circumstances that heighten the degree or likelihood of probable loss. You might notice that only two of the 11 more finely described asset classes listed have exactly the same combination of Xs and blanks in our table. Some seem vulnerable in any of the three basic scenarios (simple bear market, a recession, and resurgent inflation). Others have their risks more focused on perhaps only one scenario. As examples of the latter, precious metals and money market instruments each earn only one X, but in different scenarios. Industrial demand for precious metals dries up in recession, but they are traditional stores of value in times of inflation. Exactly in reverse, money market assets are unaffected in an economic slide, but because of their low nominal returns represent risk in the form of impaired purchasing power when inflation speeds up.

You can use Table 8-1 to classify your holdings and see if you have created clusters with common vulnerabilities.

TABLE 8-1   Vulnerabilities of asset classes

	Bear Market	Recession	Inflation
Emerging markets stocks	X	X	
Junk bonds		XX	
Mature world stock markets	X	X	X
Small, mid-cap U.S. stocks	XX	X	
Large-cap U.S. stocks	X	XX	
Convertible securities		X	X
Precious metals		X	
Utilities and REITs			X
High-quality corporate bonds		X	XX
Government bonds			XX
Money market assets			X

Depending on what appears to be the nature of the pending downside scenario, your going-in holdings might imply greater or lesser exposure and therefore high or only moderate urgency about repositioning—and about doing so with larger or smaller percentages of your assets.

EXAMINING RELATIVE RISKS BY INDUSTRY AND SECTOR

In any given market decline, and in different recessions, various groups of stocks, when described by industry or sector, will perform unequally. Most if not all will show stock price declines, but the degree of damage will vary considerably across a wide spectrum from much more to somewhat less than that measured by popular averages. While the typical decline in a down calendar year is about 12 to 13 percent, you would not want to be caught holding an extensive collection of stocks falling mainly into the most risk-prone groups, because these might well drop twice or three times as much as the major stock averages. Stocks and groups do not all act in lockstep, by any means!

Table 8-2 clusters sectors and industries from higher to lower vulnerability, based on average circumstances and aver-

TABLE 8-2   Sectors and industries grouped by relative exposure

Highest

Latest big winners (see text!)

Brokerage firms

Airlines

Semiconductors and related equipment

Computers and software

Other capital goods

Railroads, air freight, trucking

Above average

Money management firms

International banks

Leisure and luxury purchases

Telecommunications equipment

Other high-technology items

Cyclicals (metals, chemicals, forest products, autos, packaging)

High-technology health care

Oil and gas field services

Moderate

Consumer durables

Consumer lending

Local banks

Restaurants

Business services

Consumer services

General and discount retailers

Lowest

Oil and gas production

Foods and supermarkets

Pharmaceuticals

Other consumer nondurables

Insurance

REITs

Utilities

age historical experience. No future market decline should be expected to produce an array of declines exactly in the order shown, but the general sequence will hold sway nearly every time.

Some of the groupings listed in Table 8-2 get their relative positions from sharp or slight cyclicality in an economic sense—for example, airlines and capital goods versus foods, drugs, or utility services. In other cases, their market prices are simply very volatile. A classic example here is the brokerage stocks, which exaggerate market moves based on the collective fear and exuberance of investors. These move more than stocks of money managers, because broker profits are more heavily tied to transaction revenues.

Again, you should examine your present holdings when looking toward a possible market downturn from perceived high or risky levels. Note your own weightings (by dollar assets exposed rather than number of stocks) that fall into the higher- versus lower-vulnerability clusters. A fairly high concentration in the above-middle groups implies that you need to take considerable asset-protecting actions.

Lots of money in the sleep-with types of stocks implies you have less to worry about, so you need take fewer chips off the table in a high-market period. What you happen to hold when facing the upper end of any given market cycle will probably be heavily influenced by three factors: your general attitude toward risk and reward, your age and station in life, and recent purchases versus longer-term core holdings. In the latter case, your tendency toward slow versus rapid portfolio turnover is likely to determine whether you own more of the GEs or the America Onlines of the world when a market has gotten high. Unless your holdings are grossly out of alignment with your actual or age-dictated risk tolerance, no particular combination of holdings is necessarily right or wrong. What you are looking for is degree of exposure.

RECENT BIG WINNERS DEMAND SPECIAL ATTENTION

I deliberately jarred your sensibilities by listing "Latest big winners" first in the high-risk cluster in Table 8-2. That definition is, of course, not an industry or sector per se. But when people get nervous about stocks, they tend to sell first what they can exit with ego-satisfying gains. Therefore, the latest winners are usually the hardest hit in the first stages of a decline. Likewise, the big winners of the last upward cycle are likely to be trading at generous P/E multiples, and that adds to their probability of suffering fairly serious losses. In a declining market, the range of P/E ratios, from highest to lowest, tends to experience compression. For emphasis, I'll list the latest winners again as we turn attention to stocks' investment characteristics or "personalities."

Stocks' personality types noted in Table 8-3 are not especially ordered in any sequence; all contain one or more key elements rendering them vulnerable. In any given market climate or cycle, one or two of these clusters will prove especially disastrous to hold (probably those most closely related to the trigger for the bear market), while a couple of others might come out relatively unscathed. For example, small- and

TABLE 8-3   Stocks with most vulnerable personalities

Personality Type	Reason Risk Is Above Average
Latest big winners	First place to capture gains
High percent institutionally held	Herd exiting: Who to buy?
High P/E ratios	Value low; P/E compression
Micro-cap stocks	Thin following
Low dollar price per share	No support; risky to advise
Regional and local-only firms	Narrow supporter base
Export-reliant	Recession, trade-sensitive
Single-product/service providers	Perceived risky revenue base
Also-rans in their fields	Why not stick with safer #1?
Newer IPOs and concepts	Yet to prove true viability

micro-cap stocks held up relatively well in the 1993–1994 market correction. But they were savaged in 1998 when fears arose of a capital crunch that could strangle rapidly growing companies needing financing. The driving story has new aspects each time around!

CAN'T QUIT WITHOUT LISTING MUTUAL FUND TYPES . . .

Table 8-4 highlights types of funds that lie at contrasting ends of a conceptual spectrum (for example, value versus growth style). As noted in earlier sections, it should again be said that particular circumstances might cause exceptions in any given market cycle. For example, while international funds are usually losers when there are fears of recession and trade wars or a worldwide slowdown, these could actually fare well after currency translation if the domestic bear market is driven by concern over a declining U.S. dollar. But in general, most of the types of funds on the left in Table 8-4 will fare less well than their right-hand-column alternatives.

TABLE 8-4   Relative risks of mutual funds by type

International small-cap	Overseas blue chips
International	Domestic
Foreign bonds	Domestic bonds
Capital appreciation	Balanced, equity income, growth and income
Micro- and small-cap	Large-cap
Junk bonds	Government, investment-grade corporate bonds
Highly concentrated: few holdings or single sector/industry	Widely diversified
Growth style (high P/E, market/ book, low yield)	Value style (opposite metrics)
Aggressive, high turnover	Low turnover, core holdings
Fully invested, low cash	Timers, allocators
High debt/equity ratios	Solid–balance sheet firms
High technology	Consumer weighted

The preceding is definitely not a generalized recommendation for or against any kind of mutual fund because of its investment objective. Rather, it is simply a factual characterization of the spectrum of relative risk on various dimensions or vectors. The author is employed by Lipper Inc., which, as a policy, does not recommend buying or selling any particular mutual funds; nor does the author.

SUMMARY

In this chapter we've developed several ways of assessing your holdings in order to identify sources of risk. The primary purpose of this exercise is to indicate the possible extent of your exposure to money loss in the decline that will follow a high or long-rallying market. In Chapter 9, we will work on actually trimming the sails to ride out the storm in relatively safe shape and to preserve capital for enhanced enjoyment of the subsequent bull phase. We'll look at how to identify specific stocks and mutual funds that need to be tossed overboard so your boat does not sink.

9

IMPLEMENTING MODERATE OR MAJOR CUTS TO TRIM YOUR RISKS

ALL THE LISTS IN the world may be nice, but they have little real value if not actually used! I urge you to put the material in this chapter to practical use. Even if the stock market is not at an especially extended point when you read these pages, do the exercises promptly using last month's brokerage and mutual fund statements, just for the practice. That way you will be able to work through the process rapidly again when next you see rising danger.

PRACTICAL ACTION: THREE LEVELS OF DETAIL
Table 9-1 is a matrix that I invite you to photocopy. Down the left side are listed all the various high-risk factors named and explained in Tables 8-2 to 8-4 in Chapter 8. At the top are spaces where you should fill in the names (or tickers) of all your stocks and funds. Inside the boxes that make up the matrix, you can use any of three approaches. The simplest

TABLE 9-1 Reproduce and use this matrix to note your portfolio risks

By Sectors and Industries	Fund or Company						Total
Brokerage firms							
Airlines							
Semiconductors, related equipment							
Computers and software							
Other capital goods							
Rails, air freight, trucking							
Money management firms							
International banks							
Leisure and luxury purchases							
Telecom equipment							
Other high-tech items							
Cyclicals (metals, chemicals, forest products, autos, packaging)							
High-technology health care							
Oil and gas field services							
Total of above							
By Personality Type							
Latest big winners							
High percent institutionally held							
High P/E ratios							
Micro-cap stocks							
Low dollar price per share							
Regional and local-only firms							
Export-reliant							
Single-product/service							
Also-rans in their fields							
Newer IPOs and concepts							
Total of above							
Mutual Funds Types							
International small-cap							
International							
Foreign bonds							
Capital appreciation							
Micro- and small-cap							
Junk bonds							
Concentrated: few holdings							
Single sector/industry							
Growth style (high P/E, high market/book, low yield)							
Aggressive, high turnover							
Fully invested, low cash							
High debt/equity ratios							
High technology							
Total of above							

but least powerful is simply to place a check mark where a stock or fund matches a descriptor. For example, Whizbang MicroCap World Technology Fund, which has gained 75 percent in the past six months for you, would earn several check marks as you look down the left column (big gain, micro-cap, and so on). So would a recent IPO such as "Internet-Trade Discount Brokersite.com" that had yet to earn an actual quarterly profit.

The most powerful use of this matrix requires that you do somewhat more work (are you surprised?). Instead of check marks, you would enter the percent of assets represented by each stock or fund. That requires a calculator, a PC spreadsheet, or some portfolio-tracking software in which the current dollar values of every holding are translated into percents of your total securities assets. Don't forget to include your IRA and 401(k)- or 403(b)-type plans and their contents when you do this work! Use the latest available statements rather than waiting for new ones to arrive: no excuses for procrastinating. When you do the calculating, skip the decimal points, which will only take more time and distract from the major message. Round each holding's percentage to a full number—but never less than 1 percent. You will then enter these whole numbers, rather than check marks, into the matrix as they apply to each holding.

This approach will not only tell you which stocks and funds are exposed to which important risk factors, but it will also quickly show your percentage exposure to specific hazards. One stock putting 15 percent into micro-cap mode represents more risk than three holdings totaling 5 percent in the high-technology field, for example. Now you can focus on any distressingly high number in an individual box, and you can also total the percentages across each row to highlight a major concentration. Examples might be a lot of money in financial services sector stocks and funds, lots of money in items at superhigh P/Es, or a large overall weighting in high-technology companies. Those asset clusters, quantified in percentage terms, will tell you where your greatest personal risk areas lie and therefore will point to the most urgent areas for attention and probable action.

A middle-ground approach might be this: skip the actual percentage calculations and instead describe all of your positions as being either *large, medium,* or *small* in dollar terms. Those with biggest dollar values earn three dots (or Xs) inside the matrix boxes, and the smallest just a single one. Then, as before, you can quickly count marks across a row to focus in on your areas for first action. You're going to like almost all your holdings (at least you should, unless you're an incurable sick-puppy collector!). But you will *need to set priorities for action* or else this matrix will never help you actually pull chips off the table and dollars out of harm's way. It will be a bit of an emotional struggle to draw up a list of things you've grown attached to that now must be let go. However, I'll suggest ways to do it.

TWO DEGREES OF CUTBACK, AND FOUR WAYS TO CREATE THE LIST

In the preceding paragraphs, we've been working on a logical extension of the work done in Chapter 8. We've identified not only asset types, but specific stocks and funds that carry more risk to you than others. There are two other ways to prioritize specific items for selling, and we'll get to those in a moment.

But first, it is even more important to determine how *much* cutting back on your stock position you need to do.

In Chapter 10 we will discuss in some detail a gradually declining line created by the Rule of 110. That lifetime guideline tells you what changing percentage of securities investments you should have in stocks and/or equity mutual funds as you become older. To figure out how much cutting back you need to do in order to get your high-market risk down to an acceptable level, you now need to tote up all your holdings and see what percent is equity and what percent is income-oriented. Here you may run into a few special situations that could raise legitimate questions. Four types of holdings merit special mention and handling:

- Convertible securities (and such mutual funds)
- Balanced funds
- High-income-generating stocks (REITs and utilities)
- High-yield bond funds(!)

For the sake of gross simplicity, you might assign 50 percent of the dollar values of any of those assets to the "stocks" total and the rest to the "bonds" pile. However, especially if you have a considerable dollar amount in these groups, it might be wiser to do a little fine-tuning. Unless you see resurgent inflation, your REITs and utilities will hold up fairly well, so you could realistically assign two-thirds of their dollar total to the "bonds" category. If you see any reason at all to suspect a recession, I would assign at least two-thirds and maybe all of the high-yield bond funds to the "equity" column. Yes, you read that right! These assets perform much more like high-risk stocks than like bonds when recession (think possible defaults) looms. They do (at least currently!) provide income, but their prices will be smashed if recession talk surfaces.

Nearly all balanced funds almost always lean more to the stock than to the bond side. To save you the time for checking the latest exact details it is probably realistic to assign 60 percent and maybe even 67 percent of those dollars to the stocks column and the balance to bonds—especially if you smell recession. Convertibles and convertibles funds arguably could be split 50/50, but if the latest market rise has gone on for three years, I'd again assign 60 percent to the stocks column and only 40 percent to the bond attribute of those assets. The higher the market, the more stocklike a convertible becomes.

OK! After doing that bit of math, you know what percent of your securities investments is equity in type and what portion is bondlike. Compare the equity percentage to the target defined by the Rule of 110. Suppose, for example, that you are 45 years old, implying (as you will learn in some detail in Chapter 10) a 65 percent equity target, and that your equity exposure has climbed to 77 percent because the bull market has been kind. The difference (12 percent in this example) is subject to being shifted into income investments. I say "subject to" because a dash of judgment is in order here, depending on how long the stock market has already risen and also depending on your own age.

Because stocks will tend to outperform other asset classes, you should probably not cut back your exposure on a rigidly defined, frequent basis. While you definitely should perform a percentage computation annually to learn anew where your asset mix has drifted, you ought to delay cutting back the equity portion—to perhaps every two or three years, until you are within a very few years of retirement or unless a bull market has already run for two-plus years. In other words, let bull markets work in your favor through nearly all of your pre-retirement investing career. You will recall from Table 2-2 in Chapter 2 that bull markets usually run longer than one calendar year, once they get going, but seldom extend past three years. Well, use that information to help you decide when to perform the actual scaling back of your equity position.

Once a bull market has covered three calendar years, definitely cut back your equity position. If you are by nature a bit cautious or if a two-year bullish trend has added perhaps 40 percent or so, you could do the cutting back a year earlier. Never cut back, even if your equity percentage is above the guideline level, after a year in which stocks have fallen; you'd be reducing the assets you expose to the subsequent rebound if you did so.

I would advise you to follow these rules governing how far to cut back your equity position:

- If the stock market has risen for two calendar years, get two-thirds of your excess equity exposure moved into bonds or cash items.

- If stocks have risen for three calendar years, or if the two-year rise exceeds 40 percent, cut all the way back to the target line.

- If by any chance a bull market extends to four years or longer (which has happened six times out of the 25 bull markets in the twentieth century), cut all the way back to the line again after each extending year and then again each six months.

- When you are within five years of retiring, use any two-year or longer bull market as a signal to cut back all the way to the line without further delay. With a short time window remaining, the damage from a decline in the third year will not be worth the chance of more gains in a third year of a bull market.

A couple of examples are in order here. Earlier we described a situation where a person whose equity target was 65 percent discovered that the friendly bulls had pushed her equity exposure to 77 percent—some 12 percent above the target. Two-thirds of that excess exposure would be 8 percent. Following the two-thirds rule would mean cutting back by 8 percentage points, from 77 percent to 69 percent, while the actual target stood at 65 percent. A full 12 percent cutback would take her all the way from 77 percent to 65 percent.

CARRYING OUT YOUR SELLING PROGRAM
When you do these reductions of equity exposure, they need not be accomplished instantaneously. But you should impose some sort of discipline to ensure that the full program is implemented in fairly short order. I'd suggest six to eight weeks as a maximum time frame. This approach allows you the possible benefit of slightly higher prices; if you decide

on a program on January 10, there is no market-related reason it must be accomplished before the sun sets.

Having selected the stocks and funds to be cut, you could
set price targets moderately above the market for each. Consult price charts to determine reasonable technical targets
rather than setting arbitrary but perhaps unlikely price levels
(many websites offer free charts that should allow you to set
your targets for both stocks and mutual funds in a matter of
minutes). You should then enter above-market stop-sell
orders on all the stocks marked for disposal. Try to avoid
round numbers (like $40), where many orders tend to cluster.
Use $41.75 if your target is $42, or $39.75 if you foresee $40
as a realistic target. Almost no mutual funds companies
accept price-limit orders, so you'll need to handle those on a
daily or weekly basis, trying to remember to sell some when
the market has had a pleasant little rally for several days or so.

You should also place stop-loss orders fairly closely
under current prices on all the stocks on your selling list
(again, using charts to define proper levels). Those orders
should be immediately below the technical breakdown
points, and be "stop" but not "stop-limit" in nature. This
process will help ensure that if luck is bad and the market
immediately starts moving against you, you *will* take the
intended chips off the table and not hang around in hope for
a rally that just might not come to your rescue. (When either
your stop-loss or your above-market order is exercised,
immediately cancel the other one for that stock.)

MAKING THE TOUGH CHOICES: WHICH ITEMS TO SELL

High-Risk List Approach

Earlier, by working through the process developed in Chapter 8, you have noted which stocks and funds represent the
likely highest-vulnerability areas. Using those as a starting
list for selling candidates is one very good approach, but it
need not be your only way to make the decisions. The higher-

risks list might include a greater or lesser percentage of assets than you really need to sell off, and following it 100 percent to the letter might remove any exposure at all in some areas that are desirable longer term (health care or technology, for example)—which would not be very smart. Forcing yourself to sell at least some of the stocks, and probably funds, on the higher-risks list will be a good discipline. But some other approaches are worth your while as well.

Tax-Driven Approach

Sell stocks and funds that have paper losses. This will start you out with no tax problem and in fact a tax benefit from your pruning exercise, and it will thus make you more easily able to sell off some of your huge winners, where tax phobia might otherwise stand in the way of good investment-value judgment. You are in a high market; huge winners may give back big chunks when the bear starts to claw! Selling positions that have produced paper losses in a bull market also means you are probably getting rid of the laggards and potentially worse troublemakers sooner rather than later—another good reason for starting with this slice of your overall list.

Last-Overboard Approach

Suppose you absolutely were forced to sell stocks and equity funds to raise a significant amount of cash, and you had to do it in a short time window. You would probably prioritize your holdings according to your deep-down long-term confidence in them. If some arbitrary rule said thou shalt own no more than one stock, which would be the only one you'd not sell? If the rule allowed three true favorites, what would their names be? You can use this approach with relatively less stress if you forget about absolute rankings (#1 versus #2, etc.). Simply list every holding and give it a rating from 4 (most dear to your heart) to 1 (most expendable in a pinch). Having done that, do your selling from the 1s and if necessary some of the 2s. In the process, consider again whether you want to entirely or only partially eliminate some industry/sector exposures. Sell individual stocks (more concentrated selection risk) before funds, and sell risky-looking sector funds before broadly diversified ones.

Conservative-Valuation Approach

This way of choosing sale candidates relies on a bit of mathematical work, but it has definite virtue in terms of reducing downside risk. Here, you impose an overall portfolio limit on a weighted-average P/E ratio (or yield, if you prefer to look at it that way). You might set a goal of cutting your personal P/E ratio to perhaps 15× trailing earnings (always use trailing rather than forecast earnings to impose the discipline of reality). Many websites, and of course also most newspapers' daily or Sunday stock tables, display trailing P/E ratios for each stock. My suggested approach does not demand that every stock you keep must have a P/E below your chosen level. Rather, as a whole, weighted by the dollars exposed in the market, you must hit that target by selling some combination of positions. This will allow you to keep some core issues (e.g., a Microsoft, an Intel, a Merck, or a McDonald's), but in exchange you'll need to sell middle-P/E or low-yield stocks to make that weighted average hit your target.

The mathematical work is fairly simple, especially if you use a spreadsheet. You list all your stocks and funds, show their weightings within your equity pool, and also list their trailing P/E ratios, as shown in Table 9-2. Here you can see that stock B, which is heavily weighted (30 percent) is also the primary reason that your overall weighted-average P/E is above 23×. Suppose you sold all of B. As Table 9-3 shows, that would in a single stroke cut your weighted-average P/E down to a more conservative 16×. Note that the removal of 30 percent from the pool means that "70" is now the new total, so each of the former individual asset weights rises to become a percentage of that 70. As a result, the right-hand column now must be recomputed using the new weights.

TABLE 9-2   Example of computing weighted-average P/E ratio

Stock or Fund	Percent of Equity Assets	P/E Ratio	Product
Stock A	20	10×	200
Stock B	30	40	1,200
Fund C	15	18	270
Fund D	25	22	550
Stock E	10	12	120
Sum	100	102	2,340
Unweighted (divide by 5)		20.4×	
Weighted (2,340/100)		23.4×	

This approach is rather like calorie-limited dieting: if you refuse to part with a certain favorite, that is permissible, but only if you give up enough other items to get the overall numbers to hit your target.

Even if you do not choose to approach your pruning decisions *from* this target-valuation angle, using it after you have set your list will provide a useful *measurement* for you of how deeply your tentative sales will go toward reducing portfolio risk from a weighted-average P/E standpoint. Any or all of the four approaches can work, and one might intuitively appeal to you more than the others; some mix of approaches may also help you arrive at your list of stocks and funds to sell. You'll find you need to exercise some sort

TABLE 9-3   Example of decreased weighted-average P/E ratio

Stock or Fund	Percent of Equity Assets	P/E Ratio	Product
Stock A	29	10×	290
Fund C	21	18	378
Fund D	36	22	792
Stock E	14	12	168
Sum	100		1,628
Unweighted (divide by 4)		15.5×	
Weighted (1,628/100)		16.3×	

of disciplined approach, as the process will be distasteful: you like what you own and find selling difficult. But the rising market and the risk-creating expansion of your your equity position demand that you take fairly prompt action!

SUMMARY

This chapter has taken you through a concrete procedure, with some optional approaches along the way, for cutting back specific equity holdings when recent market history is sounding warnings of a high and therefore dangerous phase. This process can also be used periodically as you grow older and therefore need to moderate your equity exposure. In both situations, it brings discipline to your thinking, which will help in pushing back the inevitable intrusion of emotions that can so easily set our investment choices off in unwise directions. In Chapter 10, we'll explore the concept of a life-cycle investment approach in more detail. That aspect of controlling your investment risk becomes increasingly crucial as your retirement nears, since time for repairing capital losses is ever shortening.

10

FITTING TACTICS TO A LIFE-CYCLE INVESTMENT STRATEGY

A CENTRAL FOCUS OF this book is preserving and enhancing capital by avoiding or mitigating your exposure to recurring significant stock market downturns. In your younger years, the more heavily your overall asset allocation is tilted in the direction of equities (and especially volatile sectors such as technology, financial-services, small-capitalization, or international stocks), the larger will be your lifelong benefits from sidestepping big declines. That's because gains achieved in the form of avoided losses will have decades to benefit from further compounding. Later on in your investment career, time becomes the more significant motivator for carefully limiting the exposure of your capital. Time is the friend of the younger investor but can become an enemy of the more senior traveler on Wall Street. This chapter examines these issues and suggests ways to establish and dynamically maintain a suitable asset mix during your investment life cycle.

A LIFELONG VIEW OF ALLOCATION

Avoiding all loss seems an ideal goal in theory. But overly zealous implementation of loss-aversion strategies actually guarantees vastly suboptimized results in nominal dollar terms, and in a climate of more than slight inflation will probably create real losses in the form of reduced purchasing power. The simple fact is that those investments offering the emotional comfort of low or zero volatility also provide the lowest returns over any meaningful measurement period such as 5 to 10 years or longer. Certificates of deposit, money market accounts and money market mutual funds, and short-term U.S. Treasury notes provide low-single-digit returns—and that's before taxes and inflation. For example, a 4 percent nominal interest return becomes about 2.7 percent after taxes at an assumed combined 33 percent federal and state marginal rate. For investors in higher marginal brackets and in high-tax states like California and New York, combined marginal rates reach into the mid- to upper 40 percents, so a 4 percent nominal rate becomes just over 2 percent after taxes—but before inflation! Inflation in the 2+ percent range, as was prevailing in the late 1990s, would essentially wipe out the remaining after-tax return of those "safe" 4 percent investments.

One simply *must* take risk of volatility and of loss in order to have any realistic chance of achieving acceptable after-tax, after-inflation returns. To put it in common language, as an investor you have a choice between sleeping well now or eating well later. Once again, this is a reminder that, in investing, what seems intuitively most comfortable (total risk avoidance) will prove to be a bad financial approach.

The far other end of the investment-risk spectrum, namely, being 100 percent invested in common stocks and in equity mutual funds, would appear, in theory, to offer the highest return on invested capital. And it does—on paper! Every long-term study finds that stocks generate the highest returns on average—better than bonds, and much better than cash-type investments. Therefore, one could expect to amass the greatest wealth for a comfortable retirement experience by putting 100 percent of his or her portfolio into stocks and keeping it there. But there's the rub! Keeping it there is a lot more easily said than done.

As human beings, we're emotional creatures, alternately swinging from overoptimism and greed to fear and overly cautious behavior. We strongly tend to project our most recent experience (especially if it has been vivid or intense) into the future. After a market has risen for three years, we expect per-petual gains—just when history says the odds are 3:1 favor-ing a year of decline (Chapter 2, Table 2-2 again). After three or four calendar quarters of losses, we envision the financial and economic worlds crumbling and our savings spiraling down to zero—just when historical odds exceed 80 percent for a nearby recovery. Therefore, the key problem with putting *all* our eggs into the equity basket until we retire is not that stocks are risky but that we humans are prone to being our own worst enemies: we're likely to panic and abandon the Good Ship Equity at just the wrong time(s). The more of our total capital we expose to stocks' gyrations, the more prone we render ourselves to quitting at or near bottoms.

Therefore, for both psychological and financial-history reasons, it is better to maintain a mix of assets than to bet any-thing near 100 percent on either maximum growth or maxi-mum safety. Your mix should gradually shift toward a more capital-conservative orientation over the years. You can envi-sion this process on a timeline, with your age on the horizon-tal axis and your equity exposure as a percent of total investments plotted on the vertical axis. (See Figure 10-1.) Various mutual funds companies, brokerage firms, financial planners, and financial publications and software use different labels and a variety of age brackets in delineating their phases of investment life, but all aim at a common underlying con-cept: your equity exposure should start high and gradually decline as your remaining expected life span shortens. A handy and realistic way to formulate the concept is to think in terms of the Rule of 110 (discussed briefly in Chapter 9), which some years back was the Rule of 100, and which even this author based on the number 105 in a previous book. Here is how it works: subtract your age from the number 110; the result is the suggested minimum percentage of financial assets you should have in equities. At age 30, that means 80 percent (110 – 30). At age 50, though it might feel a little risky, still 60 percent. And at age 85, yes, even then 25 percent!

Why would you always want some assets invested for growth? Two great financial enemies you cannot control are inflation (resulting in loss of purchasing power of your assets and your income stream) and (ironic though it sounds) the advances of medical science. The latter factor, especially at the dawn of the twenty-first century, could radically impact your length of life. Outliving your assets could be the bad news that comes along with such good medical tidings as eradication of cancer, stroke, and heart disease. The recently popularized concept of dying broke (by spending your assets down to zero toward your expected time of death) is a highly risky approach. If you're wrong on the short side in your longevity estimate, you'll live your unexpected excess years

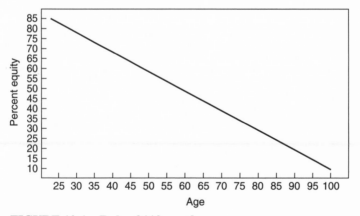

FIGURE 10-1   Rule of 110 graph

in poverty, depending on Social Security and public or family assistance. Some financial planners and many individuals aim toward drawing down both income and capital to an advanced age such as 95, thus accepting only limited risk of being wrong beyond that point. Others, who operate on the "bag-lady principle" of always fearing being penniless and homeless, accumulate obsessively so they can expect to live entirely on their income and never face any fear of needing to invade capital. It is not my place to prescribe which of those is the better choice for you. Personally, I would prefer to err on the more cautious side, although not necessarily out to the absolute extreme. Figure 10-2 might help your planning: it indicates how long a sum lasts at given combinations of annual earnings and drawdown percentages.

Annual growth rate

	5%	6%	7%	8%	9%	10%	11%	12%	13%	14%	15%
20%	6	6	6	7	7	7	8	8	9	9	10
19%	6	7	7	7	8	8	8	9	9	10	10
18%	7	7	8	8	9	9	10	10	11	12	13
17%	7	7	8	8	9	9	10	11	12	13	15
16%	8	8	9	9	10	10	11	12	14	16	20
15%	8	9	9	10	11	12	13	14	16	20	I
14%	9	10	10	11	12	13	15	17	22	I	
13%	10	11	11	12	14	15	18	23	I		
12%	11	12	13	14	16	19	24	I			
11%	12	14	15	17	20	25	I				
10%	14	15	17	20	27	I					
9%	16	18	22	29	I						
8%	20	23	30	I							
7%	25	33	I								
6%	37	I									
5%	I										

(Left vertical axis label: Drawdown of starting sum)

I = Indefinite period of time

FIGURE 10-2   **Years a principal sum lasts depending on growth and drawdown rates.**

The Rule of 110 should serve as a general guide, but realistically it must be flexibly implemented based on individual circumstances. For example, if people in your family routinely live longer than mortality tables predict, you would need to raise your target-equity percentage from what's calculated under this rule. And if you are considerably more or less risk-tolerant than average, you might add or subtract 5 percent from the "standard" equity target for your age. I would strongly advise against bending the rule any more than 5 percent toward loss avoidance, because excessive caution will considerably reduce your eventual asset pool and therefore your standard of living. Again, there's that trade-off between sleeping perfectly now and living comfortably later, and yet another example of comfort zones being counterproductive.

In this chapter, we will assume a literal, unadjusted use of the Rule of 110; you can mentally slide the targets up- or downward a bit according to your personal situation. However, the apparent precision of that line on a graph, pointing to a very specific asset mix, is not literally intended in practice. With a PC spreadsheet, one could readily define precise monthly or weekly target percentages over a lifetime. But at a practical level, transactions costs to implement changes so frequently would outweigh any benefits. The target line should serve as your guideline—a means of noting when investment positions have gotten out of proportion to a meaningful degree.

Because your intended target-equity percentage gradually declines as you age, in the absence of adding new money (almost always into bonds!) your recurring tendency will be to sell stocks and equity mutual funds and add to bonds and bond funds. The fact that equities will outperform other asset classes over time will make the need for such shifts greater and somewhat more frequent. This is because what starts out as, for example, a 50/50 asset mix grows out of proportion as stocks outrun bonds; the equity percentage grows at the same time that the march of years would point to gradual reduction in that stock exposure. Assume, for example, a starting 50/50 asset mix, where stocks return an average 11 percent annually, compounded, and bonds produce 7 percent. In 5 years the asset mix will have become 54.6 percent equities, and in 10 years, 59.1 percent. But the aging factor will call for paring back equity not just to a 50/50 mix, but to a 45 percent and then 5 years later to just a 40 percent exposure. Thus, after 10 years, an unmodified portfolio would have shifted such that its equity proportion (read, exposure to risk) will be 48 percent too heavy. As indicated in Table 10-1, an original $50,000 in stocks would have grown to nearly $142,000 and should be reduced to about $96,000 to stay in proportion on the Rule-of-110 line.

Because of the mathematics (the shifting relative target percentages over time and the compounding effects of differing investment returns), the proportional need for paring equity dollars to get them back into line with intended percentage levels becomes greater as one ages. This implies greater attention to changes in the markets and probably increasingly frequent adjusting.

PRACTICAL IMPLEMENTATION OF THE RULE OF 110

How do you stay on course? The simplest approach would be to make an annual recalculation and shift assets accordingly. However, the price of such simplicity will be lost investment gains (and to a small degree some loss of investment returns on taxes paid earlier because some of the taxes eventually due will be paid more frequently). Annual re-balancing will keep you more closely on track. *However,* because you'll be

TABLE 10-1   Need to prune equity gains over time

	Year 0	Year-End 5	Year-End 10	Target at Year-End 10
Bond pool	$50,000	70,128	98,358	144,197
as %	50	45.4	40.9	60
Equity pool	$50,000	84,253	141,970	96,131
as %	50	54.6	59.1	40

selling stocks and buying bonds in nearly all cases (moving away from an asset class likely to outperform), you will be reducing overall weighted returns moderately.

Operationally, I'd advise you to *make an assessment* annually, right after your November 30 brokerage and mutual funds statements are in hand. That way, you can readily total your asset allocations and figure what new percentages your dollars represent. And you can also identify holdings with the smallest ratios of gain to current value (including those with actual paper losses). These latter might be disposed of in December, all other considerations being equal, to create a tax saving for the old year. (Emphasizing sales of such stocks will also serve the old rubric of pruning your losers and letting your winners run.) Where stocks and equity funds to be sold will generate significant gains, holding off to sell in January or early February would make sense from two standpoints. First, tax payments on gains will be postponed by a year (or some fraction thereof, depending on your schedule of paying estimated taxes). Second, the tendency of the stock market to rally in January will provide you with higher exit prices in more years than not. (Stocks rose in 34 of the 49 Januarys from 1950 to 1998, topped only by 34 of 48 times in Decembers (through 1997).) Doing an assessment in early December is necessary in order to retain your tax-timing options; once January 2 arrives, all of the old year's choices are already foreclosed.

BACK TO THE LINE EVERY YEAR?

Should you mathematically reposition your assets percentages *every* year exactly as the ever declining Rule-of-110 line will imply? Almost certainly not. While the exercise is a good discipline, and while doing it will give you some (probably needed) practice in the difficult art of selling, you will spend somewhat more in commissions that way, and you will reduce your returns over time. Cutting back your equity exposure to meet the Rule-of-110 line will reduce your likelihood of amassing a vast asset total every time you do it, according to probability. And yet, we know that markets do not rise forever without correcting. Stocks rise about 70 percent of all calendar years, but that does not mean a neat 5 out of each 7, or exactly 7 out of every 10. Still, some patterns appear to work in your favor. Since 1960, the S&P 500 index has accomplished consecutive runs of annual positive returns (including dividends) more than three years in a row only twice—from 1982 through 1989, during which a massive decrease in interest rates was taking place, and again in the unprecedented price explosion of 1995–1998. Looking at the market's downside, in that same period since 1960 the S&P 500 index showed consecutive annual losses only once—when the terrible inflation burst and the recession of 1973–1974 crushed both stocks and bonds.

On the basis of these observations, two rules are clearly in order:

1.   Definitely reduce your equity exposure in January after three consecutive annual price increases in the S&P 500 or Dow Jones Industrials.

2.   Never reduce your equity exposure in January of a year immediately following a year's loss in major averages.

Two additional rules appear to have merit:

3.   Resist all temptation to increase your equity percentage exposure after two or three consecutive annual gains in the averages—especially if you are ahead of the curve in building needed assets.

4.   If you are playing catch-up in terms of building the asset pool you'll need for retiring on an adequate income, find the courage to increase your equity percentage exposure in December of years when the stock market is down. Stocks might drop a bit longer, but probably not for another whole 12 months! And January could bring a quick bounce.

Let's look at these rules. The first follows the principle of allowing your gains to run. Conveniently, it will turn most of your realized profits into lower-taxed long-term capital gains. The remaining three rules are, to varying degrees, counterintuitive. Following them will cause you some pain, but they're extremely important. Rule 3 reminds you not to follow the equivalent of the gambler's ruin, in which players who feel they are on a hot streak let it all ride until a disastrous loss occurs. Greed is an easy trap to fall into. This is because we tend to project our expectations for the future based on recent past trends. A few years of nearly constant wins, such as were seen in 1995–1998, make us giddy and forgetful. The longer the gains last, the more elated we become. The faster the gains, the more P/E ratios are expanding, because prices are rising much faster than corporate earnings. So, the bigger and longer the gains, the greater and sooner the chance of a meaningful correction. Exactly when you feel smart and lucky enough to raise your equity position is when the odds will have become high for a decline. There's that comfort thing again!

Rules 2 and especially 4 will be very difficult to follow. Why? Fear is a very strong emotion, one considerably more forceful than greed. Psychologically, most humans (despite claiming an optimistic outlook on the world) place a higher priority on loss avoidance than on gain seeking. So when stocks fall, our first and unfortunately natural response is to sell. The longer the period of decline, and definitely the deeper the percentage setback, the greater our pain becomes, until we reach a breaking point. That's why it is quite literally true for the majority of investors that "just when I decided to sell, the market turned around and recovered." You must keep the perspective of history: stocks seldom decline more than one full calendar year in a row. But remember, by the time you've already suffered through a year's decline, you will be acutely aware of all the reasons stocks are down, and you'll be inclined to expect further bad news to drive prices lower. You must resist that tug on your emotions, that appeal to your worst fears.

If you think hanging in and not selling after a year's decline is a stern test of your intestinal fortitude, following rule 4 will be even rougher! After a decline of a year—and those have averaged almost 11 percent since 1960 and almost 13 percent since 1900 on a calendar basis (and considerably deeper on the psychologically more meaningful top-to-bottom basis)—you will be quite ready to pull the covers over your head and seek the warm safety of bonds or money market funds. And yet right then, not only *not* selling, but actually stepping up and *buying* is the right thing to do. Literally(!), 9 out of 10 times since 1960, a calendar year of net loss in the S&P 500 (including dividends) has been followed by a rebound. Those gains averaged over 17 percent in the first year of advance. The one decline (1974) was 20 percent. So the odds were 90 percent in your favor if you could grit your teeth and buy despite your fear. Following a down year, the average gain was 13.4 percent, even including that one big losing year—a price recovery well above the mean gain (of under 9 percent) for all 40 years!

But the first-year gain was only part of the story: in 9 out of the 10 market improvements following calendar-year declines, the gain persisted for at least two years! Therefore, buying (or at least holding!) stocks after a down year would have put you in position not only for one year of above-average gains, but into the stock market usually ahead of at least a two-year rally! The bottom line here is a basic truth in investing: what seems most obvious will often prove wrong, and what seems most difficult, lonely, and counterintuitive (because it is the vast minority view!) will almost always prove a winning tactical move. So remember, you've now been told in clear terms: when the market has fallen for a year, it will be a mistake to sell down or sell out; in fact, the truly courageous move for big winnings is to fight your fear and buy in the face of bad news. In investing and in trading, you don't get paid to do what has become "obvious" and easy for the majority; you get paid to take the lonely road.

You'll notice that the preceding discussion was calibrated to time rather than to percentage drifts above the Rule of 110 line. Annual or biennial reviews and asset shifting were described, for example. The reason is that any moderate drift, such as 5 percent, can occur very quickly—sometimes in just a few months—and very frequent reductions in stock exposure back to the line will most often impose the unfortunate result of cutting total returns and therefore limiting the size of your asset pool. Take advantage of the fact that stocks' advances usually run more than one year in length rather than trying to guess the vertical height of each upward cycle's gain. Give stocks a chance to make you rich rather than focusing obsessively on a strict asset-allocation formula. Big gains should rightly raise some concern over the need to preserve assets, but small-percentage drifts should not drive rigid, overly frequent, responses.

REDUCING EQUITY EXPOSURE SO WINNING
IS A VIRTUAL "SURE THING"

If you follow the preceding rules and if the stock market performs anywhere close to in line with patterns and rates of gain as seen in the twentieth century, your equity percentage exposure will actually increase rather than adhering to the declining Rule-of-110 line over time. Assuming you began investing early enough and are continuing to make annual net contributions to your invested assets, it is realistically possible that at some time you'll be able to see wealth accumulation beyond what is "necessary" for your comfortable-retirement goals.

Suppose, for example, that your goal is to have pretax income above Social Security (and any guaranteed pensions and annuities) of $50,000 per year and never need to dip into principal to receive that cash flow. If quality bonds yield as low as 5 percent—which they did in late 1998 for the first time in several decades—you'd need only $1 million to ensure that income stream. When a time comes such that stocks have provided such sustained superior returns that you can calculate a very low required future compounded rate of return to reach that $1 million, you can and should reduce risk (exposure to equities) so that the chances of missing your mark become extremely small—so that only a depression's huge equity losses would be able to foil your thus-far-successful plan.

Suppose, to look at another case, that you wish to retire at age 62 and find, 10 years before that, that you already have in place two-thirds of your needed capital (meaning what you require to generate the retirement income you see spending). If you earn a mere 4 percent compounded after taxes for the remaining 10 years, your asset pool will rise by 48 percent, leaving you just minutely (1.3 percent) shy of your goal. And that assumes no net saving/investing in your likely peak earning/net-saving years! At that point you will "have it made" at age 52 and can reasonably reduce your equity exposure. Because there has been only one 10-year period in the last 75 years when stocks lost money (in the Great Depression), you can earn interest on your bond assets, figure to break even (at worst) on your stocks, and still reach your goal.

If such fortunate circumstances arise, how should you respond? Well, you actually will have more than one option. Your most aggressive course will be to do nothing, allowing your above-the-line equity stake to ride in hopes that you'll become considerably richer than you'd earlier planned. Careful! The more tempted you are to do that, the higher the market is likely to be and the more due for a correction. You could take a middle course and reduce your equity exposure gradually every year or two—but never after declining years. If stocks continue performing at their average historical pace of about 11 percent, your above-needs weighting in stocks will allow you to retire earlier or richer than you'd planned, since that million-dollar (or whatever) goal will be achieved before you'd originally programmed it to.

WANING TIME WINDOW RAISES YOUR STAKES

Please be extremely sensitive to this warning: the shorter the remaining time window between your consideration of such risk-taking behaviors and your intended retirement date, the higher is the risk of failure if you time your exit badly or if you overstay the crest of a prosperous market wave. Putting it another way, a sharp correction is always possible, and the worst time for it to occur is when you'd have only a little time left to accomplish a recovery. An office friend of mine rue-fully remarked after taking a 35 percent loss in aggressive stocks during the summer of 1998 that "this so-called routine correction has just changed my retirement plan: it put it off by several years."

You have no control over the stock market's level or the timing of its upward and downward moves. *All you can control is your emotional responses to the stimuli that market moves present.* You will always be tempted strongly to do just the wrong thing—to project continuation of the latest trend and therefore to overstay after a great bull market, or to quit after a painful setback. You are in a position to make the market's moves have a worse-than-average effect on you if you follow the recent trend and especially if you panic after a decline. Winning is not easy, but you do know the rules: do what feels uncomfortable. That means taking some chips off the table when the game is still lots of fun. And even harder, it means not reducing your equity position after seeing some capital having already melted away. Remember how rare are bear markets exceeding one year!

The main reasons for changing your course in an attempt to generate more capital than you originally projected as necessary should be related to possible needs rather than ego-created wants. You've decided a larger bequest to your college or favorite charity is worthy of pursuing, or there are more grandchildren to help educate, or you can see a realistic chance of living longer or with higher inflation than earlier expected. Running up the score merely to see how many dollars you can pile up will impress only you and the estate tax agents, and trying to do so will raise your risk level and probably your blood pressure. Remember, after ages 50 to 55 or so, you don't need any unnecessary sources of stress. You will naturally feel a decreasing emotional tolerance for risk and loss, so placing your capital in harm's way more than truly necessary should not be done just as an ego-stroking exercise.

THE FINAL FIVE YEARS BEFORE RETIREMENT

Assuming that your equity exposure has treated you well enough so your targeted nest egg is either already in hand or virtually fully funded, you will have entered a critical period: the pre-retirement endgame—a glide path toward smooth landing if you will—that you should devote to loss minimization rather than gain stretching. I suggest five years because a great deal of history (about the past 40 years!) has shown a strong tendency for stocks to move up and then down in cycles of four or occasionally five years. Odds are very high that once inside five years you have one decline and no more than one upward cycle left. You want to catch and hold onto the good part of the likely final cycle that occurs in the five years just before you retire. Is that "market timing," the bogeyman so widely decried? What if it is? Your goal is to make a graceful and successful exit to the relatively safer market sidelines, and you have a narrow time window in which to do it! Call it timing or call it "responsive gain capturing," as you wish, but forget the label and just do it!

Remember, as noted earlier, that stocks rise about five years out of seven *on average*. Those last two words are crucial! Not exactly every five years out of every seven. Not three out of every four. Seldom more than three in a row, but also (fortunately), stocks seldom suffer a decline of more than one year running. With five or fewer years to go, you want to catch any late good wave and greatly reduce your exposure to loss. At any time in that five-year span, if a January comes when the market has been up three years running, get your equity percentage down to the Rule-of-110 line without delay. Ditto for a two-year gain that's come with less than three years left to go. What you don't want to do is stay overexposed in stocks into the final year and then most unluckily see it become one of decline. The preceding discussion was cast in terms of calendar years only. Especially inside the critical five-year window, you will want to monitor market moves for excesses more frequently. Refer back to Table 1-1 in Chapter 1 for historical context of lengths of rallies *in months.*

Your goal is to lock down a sure win sometime within that last five years, as soon as it becomes available. To use a football analogy, think as the leading coach does when the clock becomes short: try to get the final needed first down that allows you to kneel down for the remaining plays to run out the clock and win for sure. Once you are within that yardage-and-time combination, there's no excuse for risking a fumble or an interception, because you literally don't need to put any more points on the board.

11

FUNDS AND FUNDOIDS

MUTUAL FUNDS HAVE BECOME the investment of choice for millions of investors over the past couple of decades. Funds' advantages over individual bonds and stocks hardly need reciting: diversification, professional management, probably lower portfolio transaction costs, guaranteed efficient liquidity, ability to trade in small lots or round-dollar amounts, and absence of commissions in the case of true no-load funds. Beginning with the October 1987 crash and seemingly with each market meltdown since, more investors have given up trying to compete with the giant-portfolio managers and have turned their money over to them. In the author's opinion, this tendency has probably increased market volatility, because there are now fewer players and they issue bigger buy or sell orders. The sharp rise of assets going into 401(k) and similar plans and the growing number of dismissed employees who have

established rollover IRA plans have served to further aug-
ment the importance of mutual funds in most investors'
financial lives. In recent years, the emergence of mutual
funds supermarkets (e.g., Schwab One-Source, Fidelity, and
Jack White among the largest) has made investing in multiple sponsors' funds via a single account as easy as trading in
widely varying individual stocks.

For most investors, then, funds and fundlike alternatives
I'll call "fundoids" are or perhaps should be an important
component of their overall securities holdings. As will be
discussed in the following pages, it may be that for you personally they have become, or should evolve into, a more
heavily used vehicle over time. This chapter delves into
funds-related aspects of managing your portfolio for greater
gains and, even more important, for capital protection.

FUNDS REDUCE RISK

While the principal meaning of *risk* is the lack of pre-
dictability of results, to most individual investors the word
means "the chance I'll lose money." Funds tend to reduce
risk in both senses of the word. The simple mathematics of
averaging are the main reason; the possibility that you cannot always manage money as well as full-time professionals
can be another.

Selection risk is one area where many (although not all)
funds beat holding individual stocks or bonds. By assem-
bling 100 or more stocks in a single fund portfolio, the manager clearly lessens the chance that one radical performer
will significantly affect the investor's overall outcome. For
example, one bad stock going literally to zero would take
only 1 percent off the net asset value (NAV) per fund share in
an evenly weighted portfolio of 100 stocks. If you held that
unfortunate choice as one of 5 or 10 personally selected
stocks, your percentage loss would be much greater. (Exceptions are funds that deliberately hold a very short list of
stocks and, to some degree, single-industry or sector funds,

where selection risk applies at the industry rather than at the single-company level.

Volatility risk is another area where funds get the nod, at least part of the time. The larger the fund, the more likely that its volatility, or typical percentage of fluctuation, will track closely with major market averages. This is the statistically predictable result of owning a large number of stocks (or bonds). Not all will go up or down on a given day, and therefore the percentage change in NAV of a fund will be smaller than the average changes you'd feel from owning a few individual stocks. During a complete market cycle, there are three times when a diversified equity fund (meaning not a sector fund) is likely to reduce your risk of losing money. Let's look at these phases individually.

In a panic bottom, whether it be the end of a major bear market or just the clean-out phase of a periodic brief price smash, individual stocks can seemingly have no liquidity or support. That's especially true of small-cap stocks, recent IPOs, recent fad leaders, high-P/E stocks, low- or no-yield stocks, and names heavily held by institutions. It is difficult to divine exactly which stocks will temporarily act most erratically, but it is predictable that an investor is more likely to panic and sell out at exactly the wrong time (and price) the more volatile his or her stocks are. Fear is a stronger motivator than greed. Therefore, holding funds as contrasted with individual stocks through a crash reduces the volatility of your wealth and raises the chance you'll be able to gut it out through those few final terrifying days. Also, individual companies' stocks can react severely to news, but mutual funds do not have news to report that would engender panic drops in their prices during a down market.

Early in the recovery phase, in what 20/20 hindsight will clearly identify as the start of a new bull market, funds can also be a better way of avoiding adverse selection risk than are individual stocks. The early gains from a major-panic low are often rapid and large in percentage terms. A broadly diversified fund is likely to mirror the major averages with a reasonably narrow tolerance. But if you own a fairly short list of individual stocks, you have a much higher chance of either beating or badly lagging the overall averages. The nature of choosing a fund over stocks is that an investor gives up the chance for vast overperformance for the high likelihood of not trailing the average by much. Suppose you own five stocks in the DJIA and hold them through a crash bottom. Let's say they are McDonald's, American Express, Exxon, Merck, and AT&T. It's entirely possible (the cynic or mildly paranoid would say, *likely*) that the leaders in the early advance could be five other components—perhaps Wal-Mart, Chevron, GE, Procter & Gamble, and IBM. Your possibly unfortunate short-term selection of fine companies could lead to more problems than "just" serious near-term under-performance. It's not at all unlikely you might become frustrated and sell some of your temporary laggards to buy the obvious leaders—just when market rotation is about to help your five original holdings catch up. A large, diversified growth-and-income fund will probably hold at least 9 of those 10 individual stocks; therefore its NAV will not perform on a daily basis like your five stocks' total value will.

Late in a major market rise (and you'll recall that Chapters 2 and 3 covered some of the telltale signs of an aging bull), funds can shield your portfolio value from the downside volatility inherent in individual stocks. If economic prospects are becoming more clouded, and more industries' profits are flattening out or starting to fall off, individual stocks are highly subject to "negative earnings surprises," as the Street prefers to call overnight disasters that can cut from 15 to 30 percent off prices in a day. There is no doubt that virtually any large and diversified fund will own one stock or even a few that suffer such fates. But as an individual, particularly if you have been chasing momentum in the hot groups, you are statistically likely to suffer a greater percentage loss overall if just one of your former darlings suddenly becomes a fallen angel. Why? Because you own fewer than the hundreds of stocks a fund does, so one bad apple has a more serious effect. Again, frustration or fear will make it more likely that you will lock in a loss in one stock after it has been smashed than that you will sell out your fund for one day's unfortunate but less laggard performance in this late–bull market stage. In addition, holders of a few individual stocks may overly concentrate their positions in recently winning groups—and this behavior magnifies risk exposure due to possible contagion within an industry group or "concept" once some bad news does hit.

FUNDS' OBJECTIVES OR STYLES CAN HELP YOU

In whichever market phase you are facing, and also at any time of life, you can get more predictable results with funds than from holding a moderate number of individual stocks. This attribute of funds operates in addition to the previously described selection-risk advantage. Funds come in dozens of gradations of type, style, and likely risk. Although past performance leadership is not useful over even a few years as a predictor of future wins, it is accurate to say that a diversified fund is much less likely to hit the wall and melt down than is an individual company or its stock. Funds can more quickly change their emphasis than can a single company. If one company, MegaMachine International, exports capital equipment for a living, it has few escapes in the near term when an economic recession hits Asia or a banking crisis cripples finances in Latin America. Your revenues will shrivel and your ink will turn from black to red. Great growth companies (e.g., Polaroid, Winnebago, Avon Products, Kmart) can become *formerly* great, slow-growth companies. Technology companies can be leapfrogged into obscurity or even extinction. Do the names Visi-Calc, Memorex, American Photocopy, or University Computing ring a distant bell? In about five years, some of the early leaders in Internet technology and marketing will have become also-rans or once-weres.

And beyond the operating fundamentals of any company or industry, it's simply a fact that individual stocks move more radically in price than their underlying earnings and (if any) dividends. Markets in financial instruments move from one extreme to the other, from panic-depressed levels to manic-hyped peaks—and they seemingly never learn, because they do it all over again in the next cycle. Again, because a typical nonspecialty fund is widely diversified, its NAV will move by smaller percentages than will the wealth of an investor with 10 or so single stocks.

The multiple flavors of funds offer investors an ability to match their own tastes, expectations, and risk-assuming capacities to particular market phases. For example, the younger investor can and should own capital appreciation and small-cap growth and (yes, even) international funds to a considerably greater extent than the retired or near-retirement person. And even within a market cycle there are times for different kinds of funds. A couple of examples: After a long bull run, a disciplined value-type growth fund carries less downside risk than does an aggressive capital-growth fund. At certain times, their wide valuation disparities imply that small-cap or large-cap funds will be a better bet. Early in an economic expansion, capital appreciation and growth funds will probably easily outrun growth-and-income or equity-income funds. At some times high-tech-heavy funds will do much better, or much worse, than those weighted toward consumer products and services. Depending on the inflation outlook, short-intermediate bond funds might do much better—or much less well—than long-term or zero-coupon bond funds. High-yield bond funds (junk bonds dressed in their best attire) outperform quality-bond funds much of the time, but then disastrously underperform as a recession approaches and takes hold. Individual stocks do not come officially marked with investment-objective descriptors.

You can take advantage of changing market phases. Doing so is an art and not a science, so forget about seeking perfection. But one odds-on way of being a winner is simply to observe what has been the right formula or style for an extended period (and is therefore getting high praise in the media) and sell it in favor of what has not lately been as hot. This is the essence of contrarian style and approach: seeking to note and identify, and then to avoid or counter, the fairly obvious extremes. In approximately typical sequence, the kinds of funds in Table 11-1 are likely to become more, and then less, appropriate for making gains and limiting subsequent risks during a stock market rise, from bottom to top.

As a market rise hits several years' length (remember the history of average and extreme lengths presented in Chapter 2), you will be wise to do that which feels unnatural and not immediately necessary and that which will reduce your investment fun: you should reduce the risk profile of your fund holdings. A market that has been zooming, perhaps with white-hot technology stocks or small-cap speculations, is exactly the phase in which you should pare back your technology-sector and capital-appreciation funds in favor of value-oriented, balanced, and equity-income funds. It will seem counterintuitive to leave the party at the height of the fun, but you will save money and regrets not long afterward.

TABLE 11-1   Approximate sequence of leadership rotation

Equity income; REIT, utility (safe)

Blue-chip growth and income

Consumer and health care

Technology (still lagging, due for catch-up)

Small-cap (still lagging, due for catch-up)

Growth

International

Huge-cap and S&P 500 index

Technology, smaller-cap again (better growth visibility)

Value, higher-yield, low-P/E style

Utility, balanced, and equity income

You will never catch the exact top (or bottom) but, with your degree of market experience, you can readily tell the primary scent of a market: Is it champagne or perspiration? When the bubbly has been flowing for a good while, it's time for you to quietly and cumulatively take your chips off the table. Do it quietly, so your friends and work colleagues will not talk you out of your party-pooper resolve near the giddy top. And do it over several months, because your timing simply cannot be perfect for any 180° switch made all at once.

SECTOR FUNDS

Our prior discussion has repeatedly referred to broadly diversified equity funds, and for good reason: narrowly focused industry or sector funds (and the relatively few funds that deliberately concentrate their bets in a small number of stocks) largely forfeit the risk-minimizing features of their broadly diversified cousins. It would be only fair to mention that focused funds can be major winners for you— provided you do not view them as lifetime commitments or imagine them being as "safe" as broadly diversified funds. For the 10 years through June 30, 1998, financial-services sector funds and health-biotechnology funds were the number 1 and number 2 performers on average. In a bear market or without the special demographics of that period, however, such funds would probably have acted much less favorably.

Through the course of a market or an economic cycle, various parts of the economy rotate into and then out of leadership roles. Sector funds focused on those widely varied kinds of stocks will likewise perform better and then worse for relatively short periods of time (e.g., 6 to 18 months). In addition, some sector funds (airlines and oil-field services are prime examples) will show much higher interim volatility than other kinds of funds (consumer nondurables/services or utilities funds, for example). Sector investing is best suited to investors who are more aggressive than average. And this use of funds definitely requires greater attention than many buy-and-holders care to give their portfolios. It is not for everyone!

Sector and single-industry funds should be thought of as two-edged swords. They can perform wonders in building wealth if used skillfully (meaning at the right times) but they can become nasty weapons against their owners when bought after a considerable rise or when held overly long. Because our focus in this book is on preservation of profits and wealth and preparation for less-than-buoyant market phases, we will not attempt to lay out a complete guide to maximizing profit with sector investing. An excellent book on that subject is *Sector Investing** by Sam Stovall, editor of *Standard & Poor's Industry Surveys*. It traces historical performance tendencies of 90 sectors.

Our purpose here is to identify the most appropriate sectors for your money late in an economic and stock market cycle. Not surprisingly, they are relatively mundane areas: energy suppliers, consumer staples, real estate investment trusts, and utilities.[†] These parts of the economy share two key ingredients that combine to make them less risky than many others: they are relatively noncyclical in terms of demand and therefore profits, and their stocks usually trade at P/E ratios below those of most other market groups. Oil stocks (mature, integrated, producing companies—not the speculative exploration/development ones) as well as utilities and REITs traditionally provide above-average dividend yields, which is an important factor in establishing resistance to price decline.

---

*New York, McGraw-Hill, 1996, 260 pages.

[†]Be extremely selective in choosing REIT and utility funds. Most of these are marketed on the basis of yield, and that portfolio approach is much more risky than focusing on *growth* of income that leads to total return with reduced risk of capital impairment driven by dividend cuts. Growth in income always comes at a price of lower current yield. These two types of funds are discussed at length in the author's *30 Strategies for High-Profit Investment Success,* 1998, published by Dearborn.

So, to the degree that your collection of mutual funds includes industry or sector funds, only the more risk-buffered among them should survive the pruning process you implement to reduce capital exposure as a bull market rise matures. They're not guaranteed against decline, but their inherent features imply low volatility and relative downside protection.

A RISK CONTINUUM OF FUND TYPES

The preceding discussion leads naturally into a broader categorization of mutual funds according to their overall risk levels. Here we are using the word *risk* in the sense of variability and volatility of results over time. The list in Table 11-2 is ordered from highest to lowest risk. On the basis of a considerable and growing body of research, it appears one must overlay, on top of fund type, the investment approach or style employed: value investing reduces risk as compared with momentum or growth-at-any-price investing. Thus, for example, it is very possible that a value-based small-cap fund would entail less risk than a momentum-chasing large-cap growth fund.

Please understand that in any given economic or market cycle the average performance of one type of fund might turn out better or worse than that of other types listed in Table 11-2. Our intention here is to provide a general ranking of relative riskiness (variability of returns) over long periods of time. And, obviously, performance of any individual fund can vary considerably (for better or worse) from its group's average depending on manager skill and foresight over a relatively short time horizon.

FUNDS VERSUS STOCKS AS RISK REDUCERS

While mutual funds have many positive attributes, they are not panaceas. Not every fund performs well, in either the short or long term. On average, most funds tend over time to underperform their benchmarks (e.g., a small-cap fund against the Russell 2000), and it appears that fund expenses are not the sole

TABLE 11-2   Relative riskiness of mutual funds by investment objective

Equity Funds

Single-country (emerging more than developed)

World region (emerging more than developed)

International (meaning excluding the United States)

Single-industry

Global (including United States)

Sector

Global flexible asset allocation

Domestic flexible asset allocation

Micro-cap

Small-cap

Capital appreciation

Mid-cap

Growth

Growth and income

Equity income

Convertible securities

Balanced

Preferred stock

Bond Funds

World income (emerging more than mature)
             (unhedged more than dollar-hedged)

Flexible

Domestic high-yield

Zero-coupon

Mortgage-backed securities

Income (these permit some use of equities)

Middle-grade corporate

Investment-grade corporate

Municipal high-yield

General municipal (longer maturity more than shorter)

Insured municipal (longer maturity more than shorter)

U.S. government, including agencies (again, long more than short)

U.S. Treasury (long more than short)

General money market

Municipal money market

U.S. government-only money market

reason. Even admitting these drawbacks, however, funds do exhibit lower risk than do individual stocks (or bonds). Adverse selection risk, discussed earlier, is the major reason. Investor intolerance of "negative surprises" clearly hits individual stocks but not the entire portfolio of any fund. Liquidity is another risk-lowering factor on the side of funds. For these reasons, one can make the case that substituting funds for some individual stocks is a legitimate risk-reduction approach as you gird for a correction following a long bull market.

Funds can also be useful tools that can offer single-stock risk avoidance and occasional tax benefits. Late in a market advance, you may hold a high-technology stock that has performed very well and has risen to a high P/E ratio based on high expectations. You might be concerned that any little disappointment would mean an immediate 20 percent or larger price gap, and you would like to avoid that danger. Selling this single stock and replacing it with a sector fund or a growth fund overweighted in the technology group might be a wise move. (Another place where stocks might be traded in for a fund involves taking a tax loss on a lagging stock but remaining represented in a temporarily depressed industry with fine longer-term recovery or growth prospects. This is discussed more fully in Chapter 12, which focuses on tax tactics.)

AN IMPORTANT FEW WORDS ABOUT BOND FUNDS

Whatever advantages equity funds have over individual stocks are somewhat magnified in the case of bond funds. This is true for three reasons deriving from the nature of bonds and bond funds, and one relating to individual investors' psychology and habits.

Individual bonds are very difficult to trade in small lots. A block of $25,000 or $50,000 is at the smaller end of the scale of readily tradable bonds, according to most money desks. Bid-asked spreads are wide; the number of competing quotations is very small on all but government issues; and commissions are relatively high on small lots. A bond fund typically holds large blocks of any single bond it owns, and so avoids these problems. Buying a bond fund allows you as an investor to sidestep all these drawbacks.

Bond funds, but not individual bonds, can be bought and sold in specific dollar amounts on a moment's notice. Suppose you need to move $21,400, or $17,600, from stocks to bonds to shift your asset allocation. You just cannot do it with individual bonds. A simple phone call to an 800 or 888 number will accomplish it with bond funds. Ditto for using proceeds from a bond fund to pay $7450 in tuition or a large dental bill. And how would you effectively make a $2000 IRA investment in a single bond?

Bond funds are available in as wide a range of flavors as are equity funds. Combinations of quality, coupons, maturity, taxability, and in some cases portfolio insurance are almost endless. You can select a bond fund providing the specific maturity and duration you desire and then invest a relatively modest amount tailored to your overall portfolio risk tolerance and asset balance. To get the same characteristics in a single bond you must expose yourself to illiquidity and, more crucially, to the risk, however remote it may seem at time of purchase, of adverse single-issue selection. (Also, you can now even find certain bond funds that deliberately blend maturities all across the time spectrum, thus providing a mix of yield and principal risk in a single investment package.)

The final advantage of bond funds over individual bond selection is especially important in the high-yield bonds arena. You will naturally gravitate to higher yield, which raises risk you do not perceive, in buying individual bonds. Here, the risk of adverse individual security selection is acute. Putting it simply, "yield sells." Investors give lip service to having heard about the risks involved, but in reality they focus on the yield and thus take on more risk than they are consciously bargaining for. Leaving the choices and the monitoring of future developments to professional bond-fund managers is perhaps nowhere more important than in the area of junk bonds. And needless to say, diversification is extremely important within this asset class. On average and over the long term, high-yield funds provide returns that more than pay investors for the added risks assumed. Individual junk bonds can become total losses, so here the phrase "on average" is extremely important.

One note of caution about bond funds, irrespective of all their positive features: every individual bond issue will mature at a known future date. Therefore, as the remaining term on a bond becomes shorter, its price will be less volatile if interest rates change. A long-term bond fund, by terms of its prospectus, deliberately will continue rolling over its maturing holdings and therefore will always have an average maturity of 20 or 25 years. Thus its NAV will not converge to a known value at a certain date, because the fund itself, in contrast to an individual bond, has no maturity date. Don't confuse the two instruments; you may need to ladder your bond funds' maturities to the shorter end as you age. That would be more important if you intend to live off capital than if you can afford to retire on interest and dividend income alone and therefore need not worry about capital fluctuations.

NOW THE FUN STUFF: THE FUNDOIDS!
Several available investment vehicles closely relate to, or act somewhat like but may not be exactly the same as, conventional, traditional mutual funds. These are worth understanding. In a couple of cases, they have specific virtues in terms of defining or limiting your risks in either the longer or shorter term.

World Equity Benchmark Shares™, or WEBS, were introduced to the U.S. market by Morgan Stanley in March 1996. As this book went to press, 17 WEBS were trading on the American Stock Exchange, each representing the market of a single nation. WEBS are, technically, open-end mutual funds because they can be redeemed any day the market is open at full net asset value. A key qualifier is that redemption is accepted only in institutional-sized pieces (multimillions of dollars). Because of this redeemability, each WEBS share tends to trade very closely in line with the base country's main stock index (e.g., the Nikkei 225 for Japan, DAX for Germany). Thus WEBS tend to avoid the inherent unpredictable-price problems associated with closed-end funds, which frequently trade at premiums or discounts of 20 percent or more against underlying portfolio NAV. WEBS of the major non-U.S. stock markets (Germany, Japan, Hong Kong, France, Mexico, Switzerland, and the United Kingdom) trade quite actively and with good liquidity. (See Table 11-3.)

WEBS also have been granted the unusual distinction of being allowed to be sold short without requiring a price uptick. This feature makes them quite attractive and practical as hedging vehicles for the individual investor. Suppose you are committed to international investing for some of your assets but are very concerned in the shorter term about an overvalued market (or possible recession, political upheaval, or currency devaluation) in one country. You can retain your international or region fund and short some WEBS shares for the problem country. Or, suppose that a negative event in a WEBS-covered nation seems likely to affect its local stocks' price stability. Again, without waiting for a perhaps elusive uptick, you can immediately short some WEBS shares to gain profit from their likely decline. Finally, because WEBS trade actively throughout daily New York trading hours, you can transact business in them *during the day* to lock down a move without waiting for an unknown closing NAV of a country or international fund that might move away from you well before the closing bell sounds.

Another recently introduced vehicle was put and call options on baskets of equity mutual funds. In December 1996, the Lipper Analytical/Salomon Brothers fund index options began trading on the Chicago Board Options Exchange (CBOE). Options became available on an index of 30 large growth funds, and similarly on an index of 30 large growth-

TABLE 11-3   Description of World Equity Benchmark Shares (WEBS)™

Region and Nation	Amex Ticker*	Average 1998 Daily Share Volume
Europe		
Austria	EWO	8,000
Belgium	EWK	10,000
France	EWQ	25,000
Germany	EWG	35,000
Italy	EWI	35,000
Netherlands	EWN	8,000
Spain	EWP	12,000
Sweden	EWD	4,500
Switzerland	EWL	15,000
United Kingdom	EWU	25,000
Pacific Region		
Australia	EWA	20,000
Hong Kong	EWH	110,000
Japan	EWJ	30,000
Malaysia	EWM	200,000
Singapore	EWS	100,000
Latin America		
Mexico	EWW	15,000

*WEBS may be purchased (or shorted) like any other stock listed on the Amex, through any broker, without obtaining a prospectus. To obtain a prospectus describing details of the WEBS' intricacies, contact Morgan Stanley at 1-800-810-WEBS.

and-income funds. Again, because these traded throughout the day, they were designed to allow you a chance to move before the closing values of funds are established. If you saw a market breaking down, you could buy a put or sell a call on the LA/SB basket of funds, in effect locking in a trade at a better price than you'd get by waiting to sell your fund, which can be done only at the close. Such options on widely followed funds indices might also be used to postpone taxable sales of mutual funds late in the year. Because the indexes do not precisely duplicate the assets of any specific fund, their use would not run afoul of tax changes in 1997 that were designed to tighten use of options for tax-timing purposes. As events developed, these options were not especially heavily traded; they were discontinued after December 31, 1998. (Some analysts expect that, in Wall Street's never-ending inventing of new products, options might be introduced on widely owned individual funds, but such have yet to be submitted for Securities and Exchange Commission (SEC) approval. Stay tuned for a mammoth battle between the options-trading exchanges and the fund-management companies!)

Balanced term trusts are technically and legally mutual funds. But they are pushing the boundaries a bit. They combine some of the attributes of a conventional balanced fund (a mixture of stocks and bonds in a single portfolio) with other features of a unit investment trust (a definite windup date, passive monitoring rather than active management, and low annual expenses). These funds are attractive to risk-averse investors who grudgingly admit they ought to own some equities but are afraid to lose money. A typical balanced term trust invests enough money in zero-coupon triple-A municipal or Treasury bonds so that at the trust's maturity those bonds will be worth not less than the going-in price of the whole fund. Thus, even if all the selected stocks went to zero, an original buyer holding to the trust's windup date would lose only the opportunity cost of dead money.

Life-cycle funds, likewise, are literally mutual funds in legal form. But these funds gradually shift their investment objective in a more conservative direction during their lifetime. For example, the XYZ Life-Cycle 2040 Fund would be bought around the year 2000 by a 25-year old investor currently oriented to capital appreciation. The fund keeps her money for perhaps 40 years, because she does not need to switch to a more conservative fund at middle age; such a fund's manager modifies its asset mix over time so its risk profile becomes more muted in line with its ever aging holders' financial and emotional needs. This kind of fund is attractive to investors who wish they could avoid a lifetime of repeated stresses from buying, selection, and switching decisions, because the fund is designed precisely to meet their changing needs over several decades. Such funds, yet to be tested through a full economic or life cycle, are hoped to have relatively low turnover (because investors should not find the need to sell and because only part of the portfolio is likely to be up for change at any stage in life). Life-cycle funds should appeal to investors who have difficulty making selling decisions; holding this type of fund would ensure that at least some assets are gradually shifted properly toward income and preservation during an investment lifetime. In a way, such a fund can be thought of as a wide-latitude balanced fund that will definitely lean more toward bonds over the years.

Protected-growth investments were introduced in the middle 1990s by Merrill Lynch and Morgan Stanley, and a few dozen traded on the NYSE and Amex as this was written. Like the balanced term trust, these vehicles are designed for a loss-averse investor who seeks the seemingly impossible: capital growth without risk. Protected-growth investments may be legally organized as partnerships, unit trusts, or in other ways. But their common feature is a promise to return not less than the original NAV (usually $10) at a known termination date some years down the road. That promise, of course, is technically a debt obligation of the firm (e.g., a Morgan Stanley or a Merrill Lynch) that makes it, and therefore only as strong as that firm's future financial position; that financial risk can be managed by use of options and futures. Individual securities or (more commonly) widely followed market indices form the basis of these contracts. For example, a protected-growth share based on the S&P 500 index in the year 2006 would promise to give a return nearly equal to the growth in that stock index; if the market should actually be below its starting level in

2006, Merrill Lynch would return the starting value with no interest or dividends credited.

Protected-growth shares, listed alphabetically under the names of their sponsors on the two major exchanges, could be quite attractive to an investor nearing retirement. Suppose you are 61 and wish you had accumulated more wealth but fear an untimely stock market decline just before you retire and move most of your assets into safe bonds.

You might earmark some (but certainly not all!) of your assets now for buying protected-growth stocks pegged to the S&P or another important index. If your fears prove unfounded, you will achieve virtually the same capital growth that you would have if you had kept your growth mutual funds or stocks. But if you are right about a major downturn, the worst case (under the crucial assumption that follows) is getting your money back without interest—a viable option for certain investors, depending on your mind-set toward risk and your market expectations. In the event that a large market downturn occurs because of rising interest rates (depressing both bonds and stocks simultaneously), these protected-growth vehicles will hold value better than either a balanced fund or a move to long-term bond funds would. *One essential note of caution: these vehicles provide full downside protection against loss only if purchased at issue price or, during a subsequent market downturn, slightly lower.* A protected-growth share bought at $11.50 has full remaining upside potential to its terminal date, but if the underlying reference security or index goes down, you as an aftermarket purchaser are guaranteed to receive only $10, not $11.50! So buying these new instruments only slightly above or preferably below $10 is essential to the strategy working with certainty.

Another way you can protect your near-retirement capital but retain some exposure to upside possibilities is to move most of your money into bonds, utilities, and REITs (the latter two only as long as their distributions are being raised every year!), keeping a small amount of money invested in specially selected stocks. The stocks to consider would be those of major fund asset managers such as Alliance Capital Management, AMVESCO, John Nuveen, or PIMCO. Likewise, a similar pattern can be seen very often in the shares of stock brokerage firms. Their share prices are quite sensitive to movements in the overall stock market, providing above-average volatility combined with high correlation to major stock averages. Seldom will you see the shares of Charles Schwab or PaineWebber or Merrill Lynch decline on a day when the broad market rises nicely. Admittedly, this strategy is one with above-average risk. Its virtue is that the pronounced price movement in such stocks allows you a leveraged upside position on relatively limited capital without using margin. A slightly less risky (selection problems) approach here would be to buy a financial-services sector fund, because those invest in the kinds of stocks just discussed.

As a final idea, you might even consider limiting your downside exposure by buying inexpensive out-of-the-money put options on a major stock index twice a year, after good rallies have been seen. Much of your capital will be securely earning interest or high dividends; a smaller amount kept in equity funds will afford you continued upside exposure, and your index puts will give that minor stake some downside protection.

12

TAX-WISE EXECUTION

WE NOW MUST TURN to the inevitable reality of taxes on investors' returns. This chapter begins by stating in strong terms your need to escape self-imposed tax-obsession paralysis. It then proceeds to offer realistic and sometimes creative approaches to handling taxes as well as is reasonably possible within the overriding context that the investment decision should always be one's primary driver. As you might expect, all of the following is offered in the context of first consulting your tax advisor on the details and specifics of your own situation. And, obviously, be aware of any tax changes that may have been enacted after the end of 1998.

NEVER LET TAXES CONTROL YOU

Imagine this scenario: Your broker or other financial advisor proposes a new investment that to all appearances seems a brilliant and promising idea. Just before you give your approval, however, she adds one final fact: you cannot undo your buy decision; you must hold this for life unless or until it goes down below your cost. Would you buy this investment "opportunity" with that restriction? Virtually everyone would reject the deal—and consider dismissing that advisor to boot. And yet that's exactly the set of rules that some investors impose on themselves. True enough, they do not state it in these same blatant terms, nor do they create the never-sell rule in advance (instead they back into it gradually on a daily or annual basis without stating it as a going-in operating policy).

Here's a startling thought for you to ponder quite seriously: if you are unwilling to sell any of your investments "because of the taxes," you have wasted your time and money on this book! Much more important than that, if you refuse ever to take a gain to avoid the resulting taxes, you have frozen your present portfolio holdings for life. This has two unfortunate consequences: First, you will be able to change your asset allocation percentages and take steps to reduce risk in the face of market declines only by adding major new money to lagging asset classes. And second, you may leave your heirs some only-formerly great investments that they may then refuse to sell out of honor to your memory, thus compounding your tax-fixated investment error for emotional reasons.

Recasting the old saying that we have met the enemy and it is us, successful value-based mutual fund manager and author Jim O'Shaughnessy noted in a semiannual shareholder report in 1998 that our greatest enemy as we battle for investment success is reflected in the mirror each morning. His observation focused on the importance of psychological factors in successful investing. To a great extent, tax phobia is one of those problems.

Taxes, like commissions, are included in the rules of the game of investing. They were not imposed suddenly as a new wrinkle after you entered the contest. You may not like them, but they're part of investing reality. One mutual funds company sloganizes to the effect that what you keep (after taxes) is more important than what you earn (before taxes). The company's response to this truism is to advocate holding (its) municipal-bond funds. That has merit, as do many other investment choices, if done in proper proportion. But muni bonds or any other fixed-income assets underperform equities by a large margin after compounding over the long term. Therefore, focusing on the ability to minimize taxes per this company's slogan actually reduces an investor's wealth potential—tax obsession literally getting in the way of wealth-building progress!

Our first several chapters made a case for changing one's investments in anticipation of periodic significant market downturns. Such change is not possible if refusal to take profits because of taxes is your overriding investment rule. Whether it be on a cycle-beating basis or primarily in response to declining risk tolerance of the portfolio (and its owner!) over an investment lifetime, changing investment allocations can be accomplished only if you are willing to take gains and pay the resulting taxes as part of your arsenal of investment tools. You cannot reposition assets you insist on keeping!

Psychology rules. We get ideas into our heads and allow them power to govern our lives far beyond what should be their proper amount of influence. For example, many federal employees will refuse to retire before completing 30 years' tenure because they will lose part of their standard pension entitlement (which decreases by 2 percent for each six months short of 30 years). If the pension policy said "your primary pension entitlement is X after 25 years' service, but you can earn a 2 percent higher pension for each added six months you work," arguably many workers would accept the differently defined base number and retire after 25 years if they had other interests and financially could afford to do so.

This difference in behavior results from what psychologists call *framing*—an often unconscious choice of context or reference point in which we view situations and decisions. I believe that a revised frame of reference concerning taxes would be very beneficial for many investors to adopt.

Investors set up their gross investment return as a false target, much as the civil servants described previously see 30 years as an absolute standard. The income return on a 7 percent corporate bond is not 7 percent, but 7 percent before taxes. A gain of 5 points on a stock is not 5 points, but in actuality 5 points less commissions and taxes. You cannot possess that gross paper gain in full; you can realize only the net after transaction costs, including taxes. (Besides the recently introduced—and wonderful—Roth IRA, there is, I will admit, one ultimate tax dodge: you can die, and then your assets' basis will be marked up. Very clever and effective, although not an especially appealing strategy to most investors!)

Equity investors set up their own inability to earn more than long-term average returns (à la index funds) by refusing to take gains because of taxes. This self-imposed handicap on their investment freedom (and their net results) takes on a second dimension for many who do not totally refuse to sell. Enter the capital gains tax and its unfortunate tendency to create an artificial time barrier. Most investors view the lower long-term-gains tax rate as an entitlement not to be abandoned. Step back and become dispassionate for a moment and you'll realize that the lower long-term bracket is a *bonus* for certain behavior rather than the norm as defined in the rest of the tax code. Would you refuse to accept a salary check because it is available only after relevant taxes? Or refuse to work because your income is taxed at the higher regular-income (not the preferred long-term-gains) rate? Only the extremely wealthy see such a choice as real. But all too many investors refuse to take a gain unless the IRS throws in the bonus of a lower long-term rate. The central principle ought to be that the investment considerations should rule.

One might think of selling an appreciated stock or mutual fund in a different context, reversing the self-defined "loss" of paying taxes into a "gain" in the form of subsidy, thusly: Suppose you have a stock with a short-term 30-point paper gain and you see either a general market slide or troubles for the company looming. If you take the short-term gain, you'll incur about 10 points' loss of that gain (a third) in federal and state taxes. Suppose your broker or other advisor framed the choice this way: You envision a possible significant decline—maybe an entire 30 percent!—in the price of this stock. But, hey, relax: you can feel OK about suffering that foreseen loss because Uncle Sam will share a small fraction of it with you (in the form of a tax reduction equal to your marginal bracket times the loss you endure)! Viewing it this way, as we gain a tax subsidy for losing a chunk of our assets, we see holding that stock as much less attractive than taking our available gain now. It's all a matter of framing!

All of this is my way of saying that you must overcome tax obsession in your investing life, no matter what its degree of intensity. The investment decision must come first. And that question comes in two parts, although investors often overlook the second. The first and obvious component is the possibility or (perhaps perceived) likelihood that a fund or stock now held will decline. The second, more subtle, dimension is that there may very well be an alternative investment that would rise more in the future, and you may be allowing tax fixation to rob you of that choice. The true consideration is future performance of your current stock versus future performance of some alternative. Your present stock might lose money for you in relative terms, by going to sleep or by appreciating only very slowly from here on out. Replacing it would still be the better choice!

Two exceptions and an asterisk are in order. First, if you have a huge gain that cannot be offset by taking paper losses elsewhere, and medically you can foresee dying in the fairly near future, the tax effect of selling might overrule the pure investment consideration. Second, if the time to crossing from short term to long term on the tax calendar is very short (so brief that the stock is unlikely to decline by anything like the percentage difference in tax rates), then here again the tax aspect might hold sway. But I would warn you that stocks are very volatile, and the chance that you will underestimate their possible downsides is very real. Furthermore, when stocks are up is exactly the time we see least risk at just the point when risk is highest (the old counterintuitive model again!). So think very carefully about possible capital risks before extending your holding period for tax reasons. And maybe put on an option position as protection (discussed later).

That asterisk? Yes, some people have huge gains in high-quality stocks that are fairly unlikely to decline by a large enough percentage to overcome the tax cost of selling. That is a position I would never allow to develop; I advocate peri-odically selling and paying taxes and raising basis by repur-chasing. This approach (which can often be done with discipline so the sale is higher than the repurchase) prevents a psychological tax lock-in from fouling future decisions on the investment merits. If you choose to hold that historically highly successful position, you should enter the future with clear vision: you are betting that there will be no corporate maturation process, no competitor's unforeseen victory, no displacing technology, no international substitution of win-ners, no decade- or generation-long rise in interest rates.

Those who refuse to sell a huge winner because of a large tax bite should also understand the future dynamic in case their stock does decline: that personal tax deterrent will con-tinue to exist all the way down! You bought at 110 and now it is 200; you "can't" pay 30 in taxes on your gain of 90, because you seriously doubt the stock would fall to 170. When it gets there, you will view a tax of 20 (tax on a gain of

60) as discouraging a sale, because surely the stock won't go below 150. The one tiny glimmer of good news here is cruelly ironic: this "tax problem" will disappear completely once the stock falls back to your cost price!

GETTING REAL ABOUT THE TAX BITE

Most investors are acutely aware of their marginal tax brackets. If you are not, check the tax tables or tax rate schedule you applied to fill out last year's returns. And don't forget the state/local rate (although it is partially offset by federal deductibility if you itemize). The tax bite becomes a fixation we cannot dismiss whenever we think about selling an investment at a gain. The percentage number that becomes our focus, however, usually represents an overestimation of the problem. We think in terms of 31 or 39.6 or 28 percent (or 20 percent if we've reached long-term holding status). That tax (plus the state's take) applies *to the gain only!* In fact, as a percentage of potentially realizable cash (market price of the investment in your hands), the tax payable is considerably smaller!

Table 12-1 shows the true tax impact (at the 20 percent rate, as I'll assume most readers try to be long-term investors) in both percentage terms and, to be even more vivid, as points on a stock now up to $20, $50, or $100 per share. For example, suppose you have a 30 or 40 percent gain on an existing position. The long-term federal tax will amount to under 1½ points on a stock currently trading at $20. With greater market volatility, as has been seen in recent years, that kind of loss could come at tomorrow's opening, even without any bad corporate news. Looking at it in another but more optimistic way, if you are thinking of selling stock A to buy stock B for its presumed better prospects, all you need is a gain of a little over 1 point more on the new position (net after commissions) to justify selling the old and paying your taxes on its gain. There's that framing thing again: We focus on the capital gains rate as a per-

centage, but it applies to the gain only. We should think of
the tax as a sales tax on wealth, which rises to over 10 percent only when a stock has nearly doubled!

DEALING WITH TAXES EFFECTIVELY
If you still are unwilling to sell because of taxes, you should
skip our remaining pages; your holdings are frozen for life
and beyond any author's help. Hereinafter, we will accept the
need to pay some taxes and will move on to managing their
effects as well as possible. The two main weapons at your
disposal are timing and tax-wise portfolio structuring. While
both of these can provide considerable benefit, they again
must come in second to pure investment considerations.

Timing for Tax Savings
While there's little rocket science available in this area, some
points are worth a reminder; a few creative plans, well exe-
cuted, can be useful additions to your repertoire.

TABLE 12-1   True tax bite* on long-term gain

Percent Paper Long-Term Gain	Tax Due in Points if Current Price Is			Tax Due* as Percent of Asset Value
	$20	$50	$100	
20	$13/16$	$2\frac{1}{16}$	$4\frac{3}{16}$	4.2%
30	$1\frac{3}{16}$	$2\frac{7}{8}$	$5\frac{3}{4}$	5.8
40	$1\frac{7}{16}$	$3\frac{9}{16}$	$7\frac{1}{8}$	7.1
50	$1\frac{11}{16}$	$4\frac{3}{16}$	$8\frac{5}{16}$	8.3
60	$1\frac{7}{8}$	$4\frac{9}{16}$	$9\frac{3}{8}$	9.4
80	$2\frac{1}{4}$	$5\frac{9}{16}$	$11\frac{1}{8}$	11.1
Double	$2\frac{1}{2}$	$6\frac{1}{4}$	$12\frac{1}{2}$	12.5
150	3	$7\frac{1}{2}$	15	15.0
Triple	$3\frac{5}{16}$	$8\frac{5}{16}$	$16\frac{11}{16}$	16.7
4-bagger	$3\frac{3}{4}$	$9\frac{3}{8}$	$18\frac{3}{4}$	18.8

*Assumes 20 percent federal plus 5 percent state/local rate (amounts shown are overstated
because computations do not account for federal tax deduction of state tax paid at regular-
income federal rate).

The timeworn advice to match available losses against realized gains each tax year falls into the category of possibly boring reminders. It does have some investment merit, however, on top of the effect of lessening your current tax bill. Selling losers in a disciplined way (in this particular case for their tax-reduction value) will improve your portfolio. We have a tendency to deny our mistakes and invoke eternal optimism as among several "reasons" for holding our losers and snoozers (remember all the self-created obstacles noted in Chapter 7?). Forcing sales for tax-timing purposes therefore imposes a useful exercise. You will look at every holding critically, asking that key question from late in Chapter 5 (would you buy it today?) as a screening and sorting mechanism. Those that have not worked out, unless there is a fresh reason (not just general hope!) to expect early recovery, will be jettisoned for their tax-reducing benefits. All the better: you can now reposition your capital more profitably! The weeding and pruning process will have made your securities garden healthier and more productive.

Most investors typically view realizing paper losses for tax purposes mainly as a December response—a belated and secondary action in years when net gains have already been nailed down. What about years when such gains have not been taken? It is also worth your consideration to realize some losses in such circumstances *to thus allow yourself to take some gains without the usual pangs of tax pain.* This will both clean out some laggards and help you to avoid mental tax lock-in on your big winners.

With today's extremely low discount commissions ($5 as this was written), you can cheaply repurchase that beloved winner if you really can't live without it, and then you'll have an unlocked tax position with a new, higher cost basis. Also, with deftly entered limit orders on both the sale and the replacement purchase, you can very likely more than overcome the small commissions entirely (⅛ on just 40 shares is $5!), making you feel good about the whole process. What about the wash-sale rule, you ask? Sorry, no excuse there! It applies only to taking a loss, not a gain. (And remember, wash-sale losses are not illegal; they merely postpone loss-recognition tax benefits until the new position is sold without another wash transaction.) So, you can take a gain in that wonderstock and repurchase it a moment later if you really must.

Suppose you have a paper loss in a stock or fund that's down not on lost virtue but maybe because of a general market correction. You really believe that a rebound is just around the corner, so selling right now for tax reasons alone seems a misguided move. Here, you should broaden your thinking (actually, always a good idea in investment life). With a mutual fund, the case for a tax switch is overwhelming, assuming you do not invoke loads or deferred sales charges in the process. Suppose you own a depressed Pacific Rim (or technology, or real estate, or capital-appreciation) fund managed by the ABC fund group. So many funds of this or any other given type exist that a virtual equivalent will be available from, say, the DEF group. You can buy and sell on the same day, establishing an immediately useful tax loss while never giving up representation in the depressed market sector.

A strong word of caution here: you ought not to try this with an index fund in a down-market year. The IRS, should they take a close look, would likely say that one index fund is an exact replacement for the other. You could sidestep this trap by buying a 1000-company fund rather than another 500-company fund or by acquiring an actively managed large-cap growth-and-income fund, of course. Some interesting new possibilities have been created recently. The so-called Spiders, traded on the Amex (symbol: SPY), closely (but not precisely!) track the S&P 500 index. SPY's close cousin MSP trades in line with the S&P Mid-cap 400. Similarly, the DJIA "Diamonds" (symbol: DIA) track that famous 30-stock average. These could be tax-safe substitutes for index funds or a huge growth and income fund that closely tracks the main overall market.

With individual stocks, possibilities for effectively keeping your market position while establishing a useful tax loss in the current year are less straightforward. But the challenge is not impossible. True, if you sell stock to lock in your erstwhile paper loss, there are four wash-sale no-no's. If you buy the same stock back within 30 days, buy deep-in-the-money call options on it, or acquire convertible securities or warrants that you could turn back into that stock, you will create a wash sale and be unable to use the realized loss until a later year. Leaving out a relatively few truly unique situations, most stocks can be effectively replaced with close, or close-enough, analogs. Stay in the same industry and your net market action probably will not be much different over the first 31 days. You could trade E*Group for Ameritrade, GM for Ford, one large bank for its competitor, Texaco for Exxon, Sears for Penney, Dell for Compaq, Schlumberger for Halliburton, or TECO for Pinnacle West. Another and actually lower-risk switch option (in the sense of possible adverse single-stock selection) would be buying a single-sector fund. The limitation here is that not every industry is represented by narrowly focused no-load funds, so you may not have a full range of cost-free choices. It would take some deft timing to overcome the 3 percent front-end load on Fidelity's Select Sector funds, which offer about 30 industry choices. Rydex offered 11 industry funds and INVESCO 9 no-load sector funds when this was written. About 10 individual-sector S&P index baskets (energy, technology, utilities, etc.) are now also traded on the Amex, providing tax-switch potentials with managed sector funds.

Timing your sales for tax-management or tax-reduction purposes extends beyond a focus on individual securities. At certain times in our investment lives, life events can have marginal-bracket effects; until or unless taxation of Social Security benefits is flattened or repealed, securities gains or losses can have significant tax interactions in that area for seniors. The general approach in all such situations is one of choosing what year to take certain taxable securities gains and losses. The two basic ideas are balancing good with bad income events and, in other cases, bunching/alternating. Suppose you are at a modest income level and you or your spouse have a low-income year due to a layoff, a pause for full-time education, or injury/illness. That year might be a good time to realize big paper gains while you are in a lower bracket (you can buy back the same security immediately and now have a higher cost basis, as noted earlier). More happily, suppose you receive a big bonus or move from a house to an apartment, giving up your mortgage tax deductions. That would be a good year to hunt for available losses, thus limiting your tax burden.

For Social Security recipients with enough total income to imply possible taxation of those benefits, sometimes an alternating-years strategy can save some taxes. Think beyond merely your investments and include other tax-affecting activities. In a year when you have major dental bills, consider prepaying mortgage interest and real estate taxes and doubling up your charitable contributions—as well as realizing tax losses on lagging stocks. The combination of tax killers could put you in a lower bracket and/or reduce or nix any income taxes on your Social Security benefits. In the following year, accept the inevitable and let your taxable income jump by postponing large charity gifts, taking some paper profits, and delaying that cosmetic surgery or postponable dental work. Your marginal tax bracket and your total cash tax payments will fluctuate from year to year, with a net benefit when compared with the inertia effect of neglected tax-timing planning, which leaves you in the upper marginal bracket both times.

One major area that offers possible investment-related tax savings involves careful thinking about your IRA, 401(k)/403(b), and similar retirement-asset pools. Particularly if you have some financial freedom to choose how long or when you will work full time, considerable tax-reduction options are available here. Once you pass age 59½ and until your 70½-plus April, yearly timing of drawdowns from your retirement accounts can offer advantageous tax-alternating or gap-filling possibilities. Just a couple of examples to engage your creative thinking: If you have large retirement assets and moderate income from taxable sources, strongly consider drawing two years' living expenses from your IRAs (etc.) in one year (preferably after stocks have risen for two years or longer, as noted in Chapters 2 and 10) and none the next. You could drop yourself into the lower bracket every other year that way. Retire a full calendar year before drawing Social Security and bridge the cash-flow gap from retirement assets, thus placing most of that "income" into a low bracket and lowering the minimum distributions to be required annually later on.

Here is one I personally used, and one that I've not seen featured elsewhere, which focuses on tax timing with *children's* assets. The usual model for financing education costs involves socking away money in mutual funds and selling out as tuition time arrives. Being the traditional long-term holder here can squander tax-savable dollars. Look first at the usual approach: $2000 in gifts received at birth would multiply roughly eightfold in 18 years if invested in growth funds at an average of about 12 percent annually. (By the Rule of 72, money doubles every six years at 12 percent.) Hold until the summer before Chris's freshman year and the child will incur taxes on the whole $14,000 gain from your 8-bagger. A very traditional but tax-dumb approach!

Instead, take those gains each year they appear, and a great deal of them will disappear into the zero bracket and much of the rest will stay in the low income bracket and out of the parents' 28+ percent bracket after age 14. Each year, sell enough of Chris's mutual fund to take up to $650 in available net capital gains and dividends received. Immediately repurchase the same mutual fund if you still like it. No load, of course! File a tax return for the child and you have raised the basis of his or her assets while paying no tax. Come age 18, the net tax to be paid will be minimal rather than one-third of $14,000, as in the preceding simplified example. To reduce risk of loss, after age 14 put some or all of the sale proceeds into short-term municipal bond funds in the child's name. This both cuts exposure to market losses at the appropriate time (the glide-path years to high school graduation) and takes interest/dividend income out of the taxable calculation determining whether gains and job income will be taxed at all or, if so, taxed in the upper versus lower bracket!

Tax-Wise Portfolio Structuring
Many investors cobble together a collection of investment pools during their lives and, because of the legal and title separations, think of them as unconnected. This is particularly true in the case of officially designated "retirement money" as differentiated from all other assets. Retirement accounts are "serious money" and tend to get invested too conservatively because of that mental imaging. In actuality, all money not spent, donated, or squandered ends up being retirement money, even if not all those dollars are officially owned in IRAs, Keoghs, 401(k)s, and similar special pots.

My advice is to think of all your assets as one overall total and then determine how to position certain parts of your overall dollars in the most tax-advantaged ways. There is no need to have each chunk of money fully diversified within itself if the overall total is appropriately balanced and allocated across multiple asset classes.

For some workers, their guarantee of a pension should be viewed as a noncashable bond with a lifetime income stream. A good example is the federal or state employee, who in effect has a triple-A fixed-income stream (perhaps slightly indexed if he or she is fortunate). That, and Social Security if it remains 100 percent funded the traditional way, is like a huge chunk of high-quality bonds. Suppose, for example, you have some combination of pension and Social Security income entitlements totaling $30,000 per year. Capitalize that income stream by the current yield on quality bonds. For example, if corporate and government bonds might provide a blended yield of 6 percent pretax, that $30,000 pretax annual income stream is equivalent to $500,000 in nonredeemable bonds. Your equity positions then should therefore strongly dominate your actual securities investments, because you can afford a lot of fluctuation risk over the long haul to maximize your total wealth.

Now let's return to to what are literally investment pools. Here, a fair amount has appeared in financial magazines and in the tax guides of such excellent organizations as the American Association of Individual Investors. It bears summarizing briefly.

The mathematics of compounding make deferred taxes the best kind of taxes, assuming "no" taxes are not a real option during your lifetime. If you can earn 12 percent on a tax-deferred basis and pay one-third at the late end, you'll have more money than if you earn 12 percent and pay one-third each year, effectively allowing compounding at 8 percent after tax. (The reason: you get a free ride or bonus in the form of earnings on taxes not currently paid, and the earnings on those earnings, and so forth.)

The implication of this tax/compounding effect is that, generally, certain kinds of investment assets are more appropriate in taxable accounts and others in tax-deferred accounts. With dawning of the Roth IRA age, a third class of assets, subject to no terminal income tax, has been created. Some kinds of assets belong clearly in one type of tax account while others arguably could belong in two areas. Let's look at the clearest cases first.

Before retirement, taxable personal accounts should focus their income-oriented components, if any, on municipal bonds and municipal bond funds.

No municipal bonds should be held in any form of retirement account. Putting them there in effect subjects a tax-free item to tax (albeit a deferred one), which is not at all smart. Ditto in regard to Roth IRAs: no munis belong there, because you can place higher-yielding taxable bonds there and escape tax.

Generally, by contrast, investments prone to producing high current income should be held in tax-deferred accounts and in tax-free (Roth) accounts. You are either escaping the tax altogether (Roth) or postponing paying it as long as possible. Such investments include taxable bonds, utilities, real estate investment trusts (REITs), and mutual funds investing in those assets. (What about preferred stocks? Except in unusual circumstances or from very depressed levels, these instruments are relatively unattractive for individuals because their prices are determined by yields set for tax-advantaged corporate holders. In addition, preferreds are weaker than bonds in the corporate pecking order if hard times occur. Thus, I generally advise against preferreds for individuals.)

A rising chorus of investment advisors and tax professionals now sings the praises of Roth IRAs for growth-oriented mutual funds, especially if these are held over long periods. The latter factor, based on history, implies almost no chance of taking a loss in a nondeductible account where it couldn't possibly offer any redeeming IRS-offset value. But the more important consideration is that holding growth assets in either a currently taxable account or in a retirement vehicle is a suboptimal choice. Periodic sales to reduce risk in periods of high equity markets will cost taxes in the personal account. And on a cumulative basis, capital gains accomplished over many years are turned into regular income (taxable at the full rate) if held in deferred-tax vehicles such as variable annuities, Keoghs, 401(k)s, and traditional taxable IRAs. Arguably, such accounts should focus on assets likely to produce fully taxable income whose taxation can be postponed. Ditto for—and here's the point generating the most controversy—mutual funds likely to generate capital gains distributions beyond the holder's control.

Annual taxation of capital gains, even if much of them come in a form earning the IRS's preferred long-term treatment, reduces the net long-term buildup of wealth because of the lost compounding described previously. And holding funds, unlike holding individual stocks, for appreciation puts control of tax timing into the hands of portfolio managers—and sometimes of other investors. The latter operates because a traditionally successful growth fund experiencing heavy redemptions in a market-downturn period may be forced to sell appreciated securities, generating taxable year-end distributions for the loyal remaining holders. When you hold a stock, you alone are in total control of when and how much of it to sell.

Because of these details, it appears that actively managed growth-oriented funds are better held in the tax-deferred vehicles (IRAs, etc.), while passive growth assets such as index funds that cannot fit under those legal umbrellas are better held in your personal account. So-called tax-managed funds that seek to minimize current tax liabilities would logically be held in the same accounts as index funds.

I offer you one rarely mentioned note of caution here, as concerns index funds. They are generally viewed in the context of post-1982 history in which they have virtually always experienced net asset inflows, usually on a dependable basis. That assumes continuation of a bear-free investment zone (an unlikely scenario, as discussed in Chapter 2) and is less likely to remain true after about 2007–2008 when the postwar baby-boom generation shifts on balance (although certainly not suddenly overnight!) from work/accumulation to retirement/spending and from growth toward income as their investment focus. *An index fund will not definitely always*

remain highly tax efficient. While arguably its holders are
perhaps the least likely to panic and sell in a short bear market, a lengthy downturn could eventually drive impatience
and/or panic and cause considerable redemptions, possibly
triggering realization of capital gains (presumably, under
those conditions, some index-fund managers may then deliberately sell off highest-cost portfolio shares first to minimize
tax-required capital gains distributions, perhaps lessening
the tax effect). So just remember that index funds are not by
nature perfectly tax efficient. The popular media will not
"discover" that nasty problem until it has already bitten some
very surprised investors.

One other point about index funds: One is virtually the
same as any other in terms or gross returns and expenses.
But the older the fund, the more built-up capital gains it
holds and thus the greater the chance of eventual tax ineffi-
ciency. Except in a Roth IRA, then, you should prefer to buy
newer equity index funds over older ones. Fund price per
share is an easy clue to age and embedded unrealized gains.
Actual unrealized gains can be learned by phoning the fund
company or examining semiannual balance sheets' details.

Individual stocks held in hope of capital appreciation
arguably should be held mainly in a personal (taxable)
account unless you are an active (and successful!) short-term
trader (in that case, off to the self-directed IRA they go!).
Two reasons govern here: First, losses can be deducted only
in a taxable account. Chances of losses in individual stocks
are statistically greater than in diversified funds. And second, control over tax timing of gains (and losses) is entirely
in your hands when you hold individual stocks. These considerations regarding the best placement of certain types of
investments are summarized in Table 12-2.

Other, generally specifically personal, circumstances may
govern. For example, suppose you work for a utility company
whose 401(k) plan and/or profit-sharing or bonus/option plans
have you invested in company stock. You are thereby heavily

TABLE 12-2   Tax-wise good and bad asset placements

Type of Asset	Personal Name and Tax ID Individual Securities	Funds	Reg IRA, Keogh, 401(k) 403(b) Variable	Roth IRA
Muni bonds	Large blocks only	Best	Never	Never
Taxable bonds	Poor	OK	2nd best	Best
Utilities, REITs	Poor	Rarely	2nd best	Best
Util and REIT Funds	N/A	Poor	2nd best	Best
Pfd stocks	Poor taxwise; often illiquid	Very rare Exc CEFs	2nd best	If you must!
Equity index funds (newer)	N/A	Best	Low choice	2nd best
Tax-managed growth funds	N/A	Best	3rd	2nd
Actively managed stock funds	N/A	Worst	OK	Best
"Protected-growth investments"	Limited choices	OK	2nd	Best
Shorts of SPY or DIA as hedges	Yes	Yes	Can't	Can't
Quality individual stocks for LTCG	N/A*	Close 2nd	3rd	Best
Trading in Best Indiv Stocks (can use any tax loss)	N/A*	3rd	2nd	Best
Life-stage funds	N/A	Marginal	OK	Good
Pensions and Social Security	View as capitalized but nonredeemable AAA bonds, so deploy other assets even more toward equities.			

*Not applicable in VA accounts; no tax-loss virtue in Roth.

exposed to interest-sensitive holdings. You would therefore want to reduce your percentage allocation to bond funds, REITs, and the like as compared with your neighbor employed elsewhere. That difference in allocation would perhaps force investment of your IRA-type assets into other sectors, thus forcing the holding of more growth funds or index funds or individual stocks in your IRA versus hers. Our earlier example of large fixed-pension entitlements, acting in effect as a big pseudo-bond position, could similarly imply a very high percentage of necessary and balancing equity investments in your various accounts, perhaps even necessitating that some growth vehicles be held in taxable IRAs where you will eventually turn capital appreciation into regular income for tax purposes.

Two final thoughts, regarding 401(k) and 403(b) plans: Suppose your plan offers a limited list of investment options—perhaps as few as five funds from one family. Suppose one or more are not especially outstanding performers. Your best strategy would be not to diversify within the plan, but instead to choose the least undesirable fund it offers and tilt your non-deferred-plan assets more heavily into other major asset classes. For example, suppose the most acceptable available 401(k) fund invests in international stocks. You would buy that fund and focus your other assets on domestic situations. Second, in general, I would not keep 401(k)-type money in money market funds, where only a low yield will enjoy tax deferral (and eventually be taxed!) and where you are most likely to "forget" to deploy that cash into higher-return assets.

All of this said, three points remain paramount. First, the investment consideration should dominate over the tax aspect. Second, you should view your overall financial picture (including your residence!) as an integrated whole rather than as unrelated smaller pots. Those separate pots need not each be internally balanced and allocated across asset classes. Think first in terms of the proper overall percentage of each asset class according to your age and risk tolerance. Then allocate the resulting specific assets as tax-cleverly as possible into variously taxed asset pots you own. Finally, of course, consult your own tax advisor on detailed execution, using the principles in this chapter as a broad guide rather than as literal detailed instructions.

Index

ABOUT THE AUTHOR

Donald L. Cassidy is a senior research analyst and manager of fund flows research for Lipper, Inc. A cum laude graduate of the Wharton School of Finance at the University of Pennsylvania, Cassidy is a popular speaker at investment seminars, appears frequently on radio investment programs, and is a guest finance lecturer at a number of universities. Frequently quoted in business publications including *The Wall Street Journal, Barron's, Worth,* and *Kiplinger's,* Cassidy also provides Lipper's weekly radio commentary on mutual funds. His previous books include *30 Strategies for High-Profit Investment Success, It's When You Sell that Counts,* and *Plugging Into Utilities.*